D0146622

AN ESSAY ON CRITICISM

AN ESSAY ON CRITICISM

by

Goulden

GRAHAM HOUGH

GERALD DUCKWORTH & CO LTD
3 HENRIETTA STREET, LONDON WC 2

First published 1966

© GRAHAM HOUGH 1966

PRINTED IN GREAT BRITAIN BY
WESTERN PRINTING SERVICES LTD., BRISTOL

PREFACE

THIS is an enquiry into the principles of literary criticism, of which it may seem that there have been too many already. There has probably been more speculation on this subject in the last forty years than in any comparable period before; but there have been few agreed conclusions. There are rival dogmas, tenaciously held; and in recent years there has been a considerable scepticism about the possibility of finding any consistent principles in a field of discourse so varied and so informal. On this view the principles of literary criticism would be simply a description of all the ways of talking about literature that have gone on. I take a less pessimistic view. It seems to me that we ask for more than this, and that we have a chance of getting more—at least a little more. The main reasons for continued critical confusion are first that greater certainty is claimed than can ever be reached in literary matters—positions that ought to be regarded as uncertain are defended to the death; and secondly that differences in expression, in intellectual and social tone, are mistaken for differences of principle. The principles are often less in dispute than they appear to be. I have thought for some time that there was room for a study which would show how a rational approach can be made to literary questions, even to those that cannot be settled with certainty; would extract the more useful ways of thinking about literature, and show how far it is possible for them to live together. This cannot be done without rejecting some critical ideas that are widely current, but I believe that a probable and reasonably coherent view can be reached with fewer rejections than is often supposed.

Perhaps this ought to be a philosophical enquiry, but mine is not, for the good reason that I am not competent to undertake one. Many of the questions about critical language are similar to the questions that philosophers ask about language in general; but I make no pretensions to the philosopher's equipment. My training and capacities, for what they are worth, are mainly literary; and I can approach the question of how criticism ought to proceed only by testing its actual proceedings against actual literary experience. There are some advantages in doing it this way. Many literary questions which present problems from the philosophical point of view do not present real problems for criticism. I have confined myself to those which the student of literature genuinely has to think about. I start with the belief that literary criticism has some principles of its own, and that they can be examined independently of other disciplines. I have been at pains to avoid treading on the ground of general aesthetics, linguistics, semantics, psychology or social science; and if I refer to any of these matters it is only so far as parts of them have found their way into literary thinking and are subject to literary consideration.

My illustrations are drawn from critical discourse of various periods, but their purpose is in no sense historical. Indeed in some senses it is anti-historical. To extract general principles from the confusion of critical utterance it is often necessary to say that certain celebrated historic utterances do not mean all that they have been taken to mean, or mean something different. All these points could be elaborated, and the notes sometimes indicate where the elaborations are to be found. There is a kind of presumption in treating so many large and much-discussed questions in such brief and simplified form; but it is done designedly. I have intended a short book which would point a few clear directions rather than a long one which would call attention to its own intricacies. Part 1 deals with general principles and has a fairly connected argument; Part 2 takes up particular topics and introduces some new ones that are much under discussion today. The treatment is necessarily bare and schematic, and I am only too well aware that all the richness of actual literary discourse is missing.

Preface

I should like to thank Peter Stern, George Watson and Renford Bambrough, all of St. John's College, Cambridge; William Righter of the University of Warwick; and M. H. Abrams of Cornell University, for many conversations in which matters of this kind have been discussed.

G.H.

Darwin College
Cambridge

CONTENTS

Preface   V

Part One

I   The Limits of Criticism   3
II   Two Types of Literary Theory   9
III   Formal Theory   16
IV   Moral Theory   26
V   Moral Theories and Social Theories   30
VI   A Synthesis   36
VII   Mimesis I   42
VIII Mimesis II   45
IX   Non-fiction   50
X   Intention and Personality   59
XI   Interpretation   67
XII   Poetry and Truth   75
XIII Theory of Kinds   83
XIV   Value and Criteria   87

Part Two

XV   Prose, Verse and Poetry   97
XVI   Poetic Diction   105
XVII   The Novel and History   111
XVIII Allegory: Theme and Image   121
XIX   Symbolism   128
XX   Myth and Archetype I   140
XXI   Myth and Archetype II   148
XXII   Organic Form: A Metaphor   157
XXIII The Nature of Critical Argument   163
       Index   177

Part One

CHAPTER ONE

THE LIMITS OF CRITICISM

1. We must assume to begin with that literary questions are open to rational discussion. On many of them we cannot expect to reach certainty; but literary judgments are not mere 'matters of taste', like preferring tea or coffee. We can give reasons for our literary opinions, and where we can give reasons we can hope to persuade and be persuaded, and so approach a just conclusion.

The art of doing this is called literary criticism, and it is to be considered as a distinct field of knowledge. Criticism has undefined frontiers with a number of other fields; it is not a simple and homogeneous activity; but it is unified by its purpose, which is to elucidate works of literature and to establish as far as may be a true judgment of literary matters. Attempts have been made to narrow the field of criticism—to confine it to editing and the establishment of texts (one of its older traditional meanings); to interpretation; and to judgments of value. But it includes all these things. It also includes literary history and the description and classification of genres. It includes the large general questions of what literature is, what it is for, and how it is related to other human concerns. And it has a considerable penumbra of speculative and hortatory activity intended to make new work possible or to create a climate in which literature can function freely.

These are diverse operations and they demand different procedures, but they cannot go on independently of each other. Literary history involves judgments of value: how else is the selection of works to be studied ever made? Interpretation and evaluative criticism involve literary history: how else do we know what works exist, and in what relation to each other? And neither history nor interpretation nor judgment can be undertaken without some conception, even if it is an inexplicit one, of the nature of literature and its place in human experience as a whole.

It is possible to see a hierarchy in these varied critical operations (though it is not necessary to make too much fuss about it). Textual criticism is preliminary and ancillary; literary history, theory of genres, the study of the gross structure of literature occupies the middle rank; interpretation and judgment of value are the summits of critical activity. The ultimate reasons for which criticism is undertaken is that we may understand each thing rightly on its own plane, and that we may know the better from the worse.

2. There are critics *de carrière,* of whom many hard things have been said. (Sartre says that most critics *ont trouvé une petite place tranquille de gardien de cimetière.*) But criticism has been practised by poets and novelists, by divines, philosophers historians and sociologists, as well as by those whom we specifically call critics. That is one reason why there has been so little success in defining its principles and its limits. History has on the whole been written by historians; criticism has been written by men of widely differing vocations, each working according to the habits of his own trade. But it is not on that account impossible to discover principles that belong to criticism as such; and since there has been so much diverse and highly self-conscious critical activity in the last fifty years this is a good time to make the attempt.

3. Criticism is a natural activity for the literate man; hence the number and diversity of those who have practised it. It is a normal prolongation of intelligent reading—and, we may add, the necessary accompaniment of all intelligent writing.

Whoever compares what he finds in a book with the content of his own experience, whoever compares one book with another, has begun to be a critic. But he has been a simple reader first. The initial reading of a work of literature is not a critical one. Rudimentary movements of criticism occur even as we read, but to read a work of literature is to engage in an enterprise: it is when we step back to reflect on that enterprise that criticism really begins. Criticism rests, that is to say, on a basis of pre-critical engagements. After a number of such engagements there arises the need to question, to analyse, to set in order, to compare. And this activity we call criticism.

Though criticism is a natural extension of ordinary reading it becomes in the end a conscious art, an art with even a smack of science about it. By this time it is for students of literature alone. Many readers have no wish to become students of literature and regard the study of literature as superfluous. They point out with justice that literature was meant to be enjoyed not studied, and are content with their own uncriticized and unorganized enjoyment. They are within their rights, and we may be content that there will always be a majority of such readers. But to them this essay has nothing to say.

4. A literary work is a structure of verbal signs.[1] It is only as a structure of verbal signs that criticism has any exclusive right to comment on it. As soon as we begin to discuss those matters which the signs represent we enter a territory that is shared by theology, philosophy, ethics, sociology or what not. It is nevertheless impossible for criticism to keep out of these disputed areas. Whatever self-denying ordinances are imposed, the full elucidation of a literary work inevitably goes

---

[1] So is criticism: and we can say if we like that criticism is a meta-language—though I do not know that the cause of enlightenment is greatly served by doing so.

beyond the discussion of a verbal structure. But criticism must realize that when it goes beyond this it has no privileges. So far as the task a critic sets himself involves philosophical discussion, the discussion must be such, within its limits, as will stand philosophical scrutiny. If sociology is concerned, the social data and reasoning offered must be defensible in terms of that science; or at least not demonstrably wrong. This makes life difficult for the critic of a comprehensive turn of mind. But there is no escape from it.

This does not affect the claim that criticism is a distinct field of knowledge. Criticism is constituted as a distinct field by having its centre in literature and its circumference on some not strictly definable line where literature ceases to be visible. But part of the territory so described is also occupied by other powers.

The critic who sets up as a public moralist and general mentor to society may do work of great value, but his authority to do it is not derived from criticism. Criticism is centripetal; however widely it may range it must return to literature. If it turns outward towards the social order this is an extra-curricular activity.

5. No work of criticism is final. Criticism is never done once and for all. It is always contingent on the historical process and the state of social evolution. With every change of historical phase the literature of the past requires to be reinterpreted, and critical questions are never closed because the existing literary canon is not a closed series.[1] New works are continually being added, and our interpretation of the new alters our interpretation of the old. Matthew Arnold's belief in the possibility of a 'real estimate' of literature,[2] divorced from history, is an illusion. (The typical illusion of an intellectual in the heyday of the *haute bourgeoisie*.) The critic is

---

[1] T. S. Eliot, 'Tradition and the Individual Talent'.
[2] 'The Study of Poetry', *Essays in Crit.*, IInd ser.

situated in history like everyone else, and cannot escape his situation.

Some remarks of F. H. Bradley are to the point here. 'For whether there is progress or not, at all events there is change; and the changed minds of each generation will require a difference in what has to satisfy their intellect. Hence there seems as much need for new philosophy as there is for new poetry. In each case the fresh production is usually much inferior to something already in existence; and yet it answers a purpose if it appeals more personally to the reader. What is really worse may serve better to promote, in certain respects and in a certain generation, the exercise of our best functions.'[1] What Bradley says of philosophy can equally be said of criticism.

The critic is situated in history and subject to all the historical pressures of his time; but his special concern is with literary history. It is only of this that he can speak with authority; and he has a double duty in relation to it. First to maintain the literature of the past as a part of present experience; and secondly to see the literature of the present as part of the continuous historical process. No critic of present literature can afford to be unaware of the past. No critic of past literature can afford to be unaware of the present. To write of present literature without awareness of the past is to be merely a journalist; to write of past literature without awareness of the present is to be merely an academic critic. And both fall somewhat short of the ideal critic's vocation.

But deeply involved with history as it is, the critic's task is unlike the historian's. It is not in essence a study of the past. It has been said (by Collingwood) that all history is the history of the present. Even if this is so, criticism is concerned with the present in a stronger sense. The Restoration happened three hundred years ago, and it is only by metaphor that we can speak of it as a present experience. *Paradise Lost* was written three hundred years ago, but to read it *is* a present experience. And criticism is a comment on that experience.

[1] *Appearance and Reality*, 9th imp., Oxford, 1930, p. 5.

•   •   •

7

6. A different view of the nature of criticism from the one advanced here is that of Northrop Frye.[1] For him it is a descriptive science, analogous to taxonomy or old-fashioned 'natural history'. It must be assumed that criticism is a totally intelligible structure, as it must be assumed that natural science is a totally intelligible structure. The aim of literary criticism is to find an intelligible order in the inexhaustible field of literature as the aim of natural science is to find an intelligible order in the inexhaustible field of nature. This being so, it is not concerned with value judgments, which are only historical and personal accidents. This view has great attractions (besides those lent to it by Mr. Frye's rich and well-stocked mind); and its value as a prophylactic against partisan and provincial judgments is obvious. But I see two objections to it: the account given of the structure of litera-ture, in terms of myth and archetype, is far from being the orderly and scientific affair that it is alleged to be; and even if it were, literary works like other works of art are constructed to be objects of value; so value judgments cannot be peri-pheral and accidental things; they must be of central im-portance.

[1] *Anatomy of Criticism*, Princeton, 1957; *Fables of Identity*, New York, 1963.

CHAPTER TWO

TWO TYPES OF LITERARY THEORY

7. Logically we should begin by asking what literature is. But we know what it is, pretty well. It is the *Iliad, Hamlet, War and Peace*, etc. The ostensive description is good enough to begin with. The question that has commonly been found more pressing is what literature is *for*, what is its place in the totality of human experience. Our earliest enquiry into literature (Plato's) is precisely an enquiry into its place in the totality of human experience.[1] Little is said about the nature of literature in itself, or its internal constitution. What matters first is whether literature matters at all, and in what ways. And it is not inappropriate to start from Plato's position (though we should be unwise to accept his answers or even his way of formulating the argument) for until we have satisfied ourselves to some degree about his questions the others are not worth asking. Immediately after Plato we have another enquiry (Aristotle's) into what literature is and how it works.[2] This is more to the practical critic's purpose than anything in Plato, but it assumes in some sense that Plato's enquiry has already taken place.

Plato does, it is true, also report his findings on what literature is in itself. It is an imitation (*Rep.* X): it is the record of an unreliable inspiration, divine but allied to madness (*Ion*). But these are summary and tendentious arguments, while a longer and far more patient argument is devoted to the effects of literature on the character and emotions of those who experience it. Aristotle does suggest how one kind of literature (tragedy) affects our total psychic economy, and we can extrapolate from this and suppose that similar accounts

[1] *Republic*, III, 386–402; X, 595–608; *Ion*; *Laws*, II, 653–6; VII, 810–12.
[2] *Poetics*; *Rhetoric*, I, 1, 2.

9

could be given of the effects of other literary forms. But the mention of this psychological and moral effect (catharsis) is summary in the extreme and remains imperfectly explained.[1] The weight of his enquiry falls on the internal structure of literature.

This suggests that those who are concerned primarily with what literature *is for* tend to have only a feeble and unanalysed notion of what it *is*; those who are concerned primarily with what it *is* tend to have only a feeble and unanalysed notion of what it *is for*. The first see literature as part of human activity in general, but care little about how it works in itself. The others see literature as a self-contained activity, with its own methods and its own ends.

8. These two theories, or types of theory, appear as soon as literature attains self-consciousness; and they have remained fundamental ever since.

Three relations between them are frequent:

(a) The two can exist separately, without awareness of each other—as in my schooldays, when 'She dwelt among untrodden ways' was the precious life-blood of a master-spirit and also an example of Common Measure.

(b) The two can coexist inertly and without mutual reaction—as with the catharsis doctrine and the formal parts of Aristotle's theory of tragedy. They appear in the same discourse, they could have been related and perhaps were meant to be, but in fact they never are, the wires have not been hooked up.

(c) The two can coexist in a state of crass opposition—as when an art-for-art's sake doctrine flaunts itself in opposition to the prevailing morality; e.g. in Gautier's Preface to *Mademoiselle de Maupin*.

[1] *Poetics*, 6; *Politics*, V (VIII), 7, 1341–2.

9. We need convenient names for these two types of literary theory; let us call them the moral and the formal. 'Moral' does not imply adherence to any particular moral code, not even to 'Western values' or the *consensus gentium*. The theory behind Sartre's *Saint Genet* is a moral theory; it canonizes a writer who celebrates the lives of thieves, murderers and homosexual prostitutes: i.e. 'moral' includes immoral. 'Formal' does not imply adherence to any particular notion of literary form: Ezra Pound's literary theory is largely formal: yet he sets himself to break up most of the traditional metres and structures, and finally writes the *Cantos*: i.e. 'formal' includes informal. Moral theories are those that see literature as a contributory part of total human activity, and value and explain it by reference to this totality. Formal theories are those that see literature as a more or less autonomous realm with its own procedure and its own ends.

These two divide the field between them, from the Greeks to our own day. Plato considers the use of literature in the education of the guardians; Aristotle analyses the proper structure of the tragic plot. Shelley assigns to literature a glorious part in the regeneration of humanity; Gautier says it is quite useless. 'Socialist realism' works to bring on the classless society; 'Bourgeois formalism' elaborates its structures of myth or diction. These are individual instances of the same broad dichotomy.[1]

It is the moral theory that has had the greatest weight of opinion behind it, from the beginning. This implies nothing about its truth or falsity—only that it has been found more natural to talk of literature in moral than in formal terms. For the moral theorist there is no realm of the exclusively aesthetic; he speaks of literature as he would speak of any other human activity, and in the same language. Plato speaks of men laughing, weeping, showing resolution or effeminacy; and of a carpenter making a bed. Aristotle needs technical terms, or words used in special senses—catharsis, peripeteia, etc. The criticism of the common reader is generally moral

---

[1] Shelley, *Defence of Poetry*; Gautier, Preface to *Mlle de Maupin*; Trotsky, *Literature and Revolution*; Lukacs, *Studies in European Realism*.

criticism, or a disguised form of it. The common reader has not the slightest difficulty in understanding Plato's objections to Homer's tales of the gods; or Johnson's assents and dubieties over Shakespeare's ethics; or Tolstoy's condemnation of fashionable fiction. He is much less likely to understand what Aristotle meant by saying that poetry is more philosophical than history.[1] The whole to which Plato, Johnson and Tolstoy tacitly refer is a whole which is familiar to all —the whole of a man's moral and social experience. The whole to which Aristotle refers (and Gautier, and any formalist we like to mention, say A. C. Bradley[2]), τὰ καθόλου, is a more recondite object—not only 'the universal' as Renaissance and some nineteenth-century critics rendered it, but also an aesthetic whole, a thing made according to the principles of formal integrity.

10. Formal theories are very late in making their appearance. In early criticism it is not strictly appropriate to talk of formal theories of literature as such, only of writers who have formal interests. It is only with Baumgarten and Kantian aesthetics[3] that the formal point of view becomes sufficiently explicit and self-aware to amount to a theory of literature. Formal theories are the more sophisticated. They are held only by philosophers, aestheticians and a certain kind of artists. Moral theories too are held by philosophers, aestheticians and artists; but they are held also by plain men.

Formal theories can be expressed, led up to or hinted at in a great variety of ways. Literature is 'heterocosmic', it creates another world with its own self-consistent laws (Baumgarten). It shows 'purposiveness without purpose', and is the object of a purely disinterested contemplation (Kant). Its

[1] Johnson, *Preface to Shakespeare*; Tolstoy, *What is Art?*; Aristotle, *Poetics*, 9.
[2] A. C. Bradley, 'Poetry for Poetry's Sake', in *Oxford Lectures on Poetry*.
[3] A. G. Baumgarten, *Meditationes philosophicae de nonnullis ad poema pertinentibus* (1733), with translation by Aschenbrenner and Holter, Berkeley, 1954; Kant, *Critique of Judgment*.

poetical value is entirely distinct from any instrumental value it may have (Bradley). It is a self-contained mythic structure (Northrop Frye).[1]

11. It is quite possible to hold a formal theory and to hold also that literature should be subject to external control—by religion, by law, by the moral sense of the community. All that is necessary to a formal theory is to hold that these moral controls *are* external and do not affect literary value. Some formal theories (those that get tagged with the label 'art for art's sake') tend to have a strain of moral antinomianism about them: but this is inessential. It is a mistake to associate formal theories with any particular moral attitude. Maritain holds a formal theory but also holds that literature and the other arts are subject to the negative control of morality and religion. Discounting the circumambient *bondieuserie* his writing affords a particularly clear formula for this attitude. *L'art a pour seule fin l'œuvre elle-même et sa beauté. Mais pour l'homme qui opère, l'œuvre entre elle-même dans la ligne de la moralité.*[2] The car is free to do 130 m.p.h. but the driver is under the law and is only allowed to do 55. A scholastic distinction indeed. There is an absolute disjunction between the *fin de l'art* and the *fin de l'homme,* and no means of relating them is suggested.

It is equally possible to hold a moral theory and to admit formal consideration as subordinate factors. All that is necessary to a moral theory is to hold that the value of a literary work is ultimately judged by its contribution to man's experience as a whole, his moral development, society or historical progress. Moral theories are compatible with a preference for any kind of literary form.

[1] Northrop Frye, op. cit. But I am doubtful whether Frye's theory is a purely formal one.

[2] J. Maritain, *Art et Scolastique*, Paris, 1927, p. 120.

. . .

12. It is hardly possible to maintain a formal theory without using, tacitly or openly, moral considerations as a support. The professional immoralists (Gautier, Wilde) are merely advocating another code of morals. Those like Bradley who hold that the poetic experience is a good in itself do not exclude the possibility that it takes its place in a moral or social hierarchy of goods, and have probably convinced themselves that it has some such place, or it would hardly be worth the trouble they are prepared to take over it. And it is not possible to maintain a moral theory without calling on formal considerations. The value of a literary work is to be judged by its contribution to the whole moral life; but if we are to remain within the scope of literary discussion it is first necessary to show that the object discussed *is* a work of literature—and this cannot be done without using formal arguments.

Formal theories developed in isolation reduce literature to insignificance. Moral theories developed in isolation cease to be literary theories and become contributions to social hygiene. So it is a mistake to do what is so often done—to consider moral and formal theories as merely contradictory. Not only can we say that a dialogue should occur between them; a dialogue does in some sense always occur between them, though the nature of this exchange is not always recognized, and one side or the other may be virtually suppressed.

13. A fourth relation then, and a more fruitful one, is possible between the two types of criticism, besides the three mentioned in 8. It is an open dialogue. The enquirer into what literature is for seeks to complete his enquiry by moving inward towards the centre—what it is. The enquirer into what literature is seeks to complete his enquiry by moving outwards towards the totality of human experience—what it is

for. This is a dialectical relation.[1] It should result in a critical synthesis by which it is possible to discuss, in the same discourse and in compatible terms, both the essence of literature and its function, both what it is and what it is for.

But we must first consider the case of each participant in the dialogue separately. Since formal theory is the simpler of the two we shall reverse the historical order and allow it to speak first.

[1] 'When I hear the word dialectic I reach for Occam's razor' (William Righter). But we can use the idea of dialectical thinking without invoking too much of the Hegelian or Marxist paraphernalia. 'Dialectic—the process of thought by which contradictions are seen to merge themselves in a higher truth which comprehends them' (O.E.D.).

CHAPTER THREE

FORMAL THEORY

14. At the highest level of abstraction formal theory is very simply stated: art has only one law—the proper perfection of the work itself. But each art has its own medium. That of literature is language; and language represents things, persons, actions, emotions, and the structural relations between them. What can be the law of perfection for material so directly mimetic of the whole of human experience? Can it be other than the law that governs this experience—moral and social law? Moral theory says no, it cannot be other. Formal theory says yes, it is other; there is a law of perfection for literature distinct from moral and social law. It is then required of formal theory that it shall tell us, as precisely as possible, what the law is. We put the question; and at first all we hear in reply is a babel of diverse answers. Disentangle them and set them in chronological order, and we have a history of literary taste from Aristotle to Valéry. This still remains a confusion.

15. Far more than moral theory, formal theory has been expressed in diverse and partial states. It has manifested itself chiefly in its particular applications. No one of these is universally valid, though many of them claim to be. The Aristotelian formula for the tragic plot; neo-classic demands for decorum and the three unities; A. W. Schlegel's and Coleridge's preference for 'organic' over 'mechanic' form; Henry James's structural exigences for the novel; various notions of poetic diction—that poetry should never be written

in the language of the age, that it should always be written in the language of the age; even certain metrical systems: each of these is a demand for a certain kind of formal perfection. We have to look behind this bewildering array of particulars for the general principles of formal perfection in itself.

16. The difficulty with formal theory is to find the principles behind innumerable special pleadings. But they can be found. There are three such principles. They are, to use a scholastic terminology, *integritas, consonantia, claritas*—integrity, consonance and radiance.[1] *Integritas* can be translated literally. *Consonantia* could be rendered as 'coherence' and is equated by St. Thomas with *debita proportio*; so I retain 'consonance' as covering both shades of meaning. 'Clarity' will not do for *claritas*, as in English it generally means 'perspicuity', while the sense required here is 'brightness', 'effulgence'. I have used 'radiance', and will indicate what I mean by it.

(a) Integrity—the almost universal requirement that the work shall be a whole, not a slice, a chunk, a collection or a heap. This principle is invoked throughout literary history, from Aristotle to the 'organic form' theories of modern criticism. Aristotle: the action that is complete, has a beginning, a middle and an end, and is of a size that can be grasped in a single act of apprehension. (No need to illustrate the Horatian, Renaissance and neo-classic variations of this.) Baumgarten: the self-consistent heterocosm. German Romantic critics, and Coleridge: the many metaphors that present the poem as something growing to its own immanent form, like a plant. Henry James: his devotion to 'a deep-breathing economy and organic form', his objection to 'fluid puddings'.

But we must not think of this integrity in purely Aristotelian and structural terms. A literary work may be a whole

---

[1] *Summ. Theol.*, i, q. 5, a. 4, ad 1.

by unity of theme or mood—the typical kind of unity for Romantic and Symbolist works. Even such works may turn out to have a concealed plot; but their unity does not primarily depend on it. In such cases *integritas* slides over imperceptibly into *consonantia*.

(b) Consonance—the demand for coherence and proportion, the Coleridgean demand that the work 'shall contain in itself the reason why it is so and not otherwise'. This includes proportion in the quantitative sense—an important development must be sufficiently prepared, what is prepared must be sufficiently developed when it arrives; and proportion in the qualitative sense—the right degree of emphasis on the several parts, corresponding to tonal relations in a painting. A thing may be a whole (have integrity) but still be an ill-proportioned or ill-balanced whole. Shylock, the weight of whose passion is so much greater than that of the protagonists, goes near to upsetting the proportions of *The Merchant of Venice*.

Again, this consonance must not be seen in purely structural terms. It includes congruousness of imagery; maintenance of a consistent relation to reality (no unexplained switches from 'realistic' to 'symbolical' presentation); harmony of emotional tone, or if discord, a planned discord.

Consonance generally implies an active reconciliation of diverse elements, not a passive uniformity. Ironic and satiric literature makes much use of harsh juxtapositions, clashes of feeling and tone, sometimes violent. They are to be regarded as contained within the whole, discords within an ultimate harmony, distinct from mere excrescences and mistakes. Since the ironic and satiric modes are dominant in present literature many modern critics have an obsessional interest in the element of conflict, discord, dissonance, as though it were a value in itself; and they emphasize it at the expense of the harmony and unity in which it should be included. The recent overvaluation of 'tension' and 'paradox' is an example of this.

'Only so much of that fundament of existence, of the Dionysian "Urgrund" of the world is allowed to enter the consciousness of the human individual as can be overcome by the Apollonian force of transfiguration so that these two forces of art creation must unfold their powers in strict mutual proportion, according to the eternal law of justice.'[1]

(c) Radiance—the requirement that literature (as distinct from other forms of verbal communication) shall satisfy and illuminate by its verbal surface, by what John Crowe Ransom calls its texture. Here we find ourselves speaking in metaphor; but in criticism we cannot get on without metaphor. By radiance we mean (it is best to get this over) all that those who deal in 'pure poetry' call 'magic'; all that gets lost in translation; all that is comprised in the aesthetic organization of the linguistic surface; all that goes beyond a utilitarian or simply expressive use of words. This concept lurks behind Mallarmé's *majestueuse idée inconsciente, à savoir que la forme appelée vers est simplement elle-même la littérature; que vers il y a sitôt que s'accentue la diction, rhythme dès que style.*[2] Radiance can exist in any degree from the highest to the lowest, and any degree of it may be appropriate. At the highest and most isolated (Rimbaud, *O saisons, ô châteaux*) we have the nearest approach that can be made to that ideal limit 'pure poetry'. At the lowest and most mixed we have something that is hardly literature at all (reporting or the most pedestrian fiction). But some degree of this quality there must be in anything that can be recognized as literature—even in a novel by C. P. Snow.

Everything that formal theory has to say about literature can be brought under one of these three heads.

17. What is said above represents the traditional mode of formal criticism, Scholastic in formulation and Aristotelian in remote origin. Everything that formal criticism has to say *can* be brought under its three heads; but there are cases where this can be done only with some straining. To look at the work of literature in the way we have just indicated is to

[1] Nietzsche, *Birth of Tragedy*.
[2] Mallarmé, 'Crise de vers', *Œuvres*, Pleiade edn., p. 361.

regard it as a finished artefact. And so it is; and this is why these principles can be regarded as universal. But there are kinds of literature where the reader's attention is most forcibly called not to the finished product but to the continuous experience. And if not other kinds, there are yet occasions where attention is called to certain focal points, moments of illumination, epiphanies. Other varieties of formal criticism may therefore be developed, which will consider works of literature from these points of view.

To be sure, the continuous experience of reading the work must some time come to an end; and the end cannot be entirely arbitrary. The epiphanies or moments of illumination must be contained within a total form. So there is always the possibility of dealing with these phenomena by the Scholastic and Aristotelian methods. But we may well feel a sense of inappropriateness in doing so. We may feel that our active apprehension of the work is really proceeding in another way. We must therefore consider alternative lines of approach that formal criticism may use in such cases.

18. The first of these concerns literature as continuous experience, and a classic case of worry about it occurs in connection with the Renaissance epic—the criticism that clustered round Ariosto, Trissino and Tasso. The *Orlando Furioso* has no clear beginning, and it has neither a single hero nor a single plot. No amount of straining could credit such a work with an Aristotelian structure; and as the sixteenth century advanced and neo-classic principles hardened this caused some critical consternation. Ariosto was obviously a delightful writer, enjoyed by everyone. How could this pleasure be justified? A debate ensued in which Cinthio, Minturno, Tasso and many others took part.

Cinthio as a champion of Ariosto outlines the notion of a loosely episodic literary structure which he calls the romance.[1]

[1] *Discorso intorno al comporre dei Romanzi*, Venice, 1554, pp. 60–69.

It is more akin to Ovid's *Metamorphoses* than to Homer and Virgil; and if we must compare it to the ancient epics it is more like the *Odyssey* than the *Iliad*. Its structural principle is the 'interweaving' of diverse themes, and it can therefore admit a great variety of characters. It is tolerant of digressions and may comprise many actions and the actions of many men.

Cinthio is feeling for the description of a fictional structure which can comprehend great diversity, but still is a structure not a muddle, still has its own kind of integrity and does not merely fall apart. In an extremely intelligent passage he tells us what the underlying principle is. The convention of the romance is that of oral narration. The short cantos represent the length of a single auditory sitting. Each in itself is incomplete, like an instalment of a serial story, and the breaks in the narrative line are a device to keep interest and curiosity on the alert. The pattern, that is to say, is deliberately based on continuous experience rather than on a survey of the finished product.

The same could be said, *mutatis mutandis*, of such a capricious and discursive work as *Tristram Shandy*, or an episodic tale such as *Pickwick*. Any adequate conception of integrity must allow for works such as these; and it is clear that there will always be a great deal of casuistry to be done in explaining the structure of works which we feel to have a structure but which do not fit into traditional or conventional schemes: Shakespeare is a forest instead of a formal garden; there is 'organic' as well as 'mechanic' form; and so on.

19. It is to be suspected that another principle, not so far mentioned, enters into the consideration of works of this class. It is simply that of *interest*. Such works as *Orlando Furioso* and *Tristram Shandy* function by continually arousing interest rather than by the expectation of a completed form. This

sounds feeble, as though one were to describe vintage port as refreshing; it may seem not a very elevated literary criterion, since literature shares it with *Paris-Match* and the daily paper; but it is none the less real. And it becomes most prominent in those works where the reader's attention is called most especially to the continuous experience of reading. A Greek tragedy can be platitudinous and sententious in parts, and can afford to be, because it arouses the powerful expectation that a total form is moving rapidly to its completion. Byron's *Don Juan* must be interesting all the time because we do not know where it is going; and in the event it turns out not to be going anywhere.

If we are to return to our former terminology, the literature of continuous experience relies more on consonance than integrity. This may seem implausible, since such works are often capricious in development and include extremely diverse material. But a closer examination will I think show that it is true. The heroic, the sceptical and the merely ribald elements in *Orlando Furioso* may on first consideration seem incongruous; but we have a strong sense that they all belong in *Orlando Furioso*. Similarly with the organization of *Tristram Shandy*. The temperament of the author, mediated by his personal style, produces a valid coherence which supplies the place of integrity based on a defined external form. Where the strong sense of stylistic and temperamental congruity is less evident, as in *Wilhelm Meister*, the work tends to fall apart.

There is a parallel to this situation in the abandonment of an obviously recognizable *Gestalt* in much modern painting— abstract impressionism, 'action painting', etc. The principle of unity here is something like the personal handwriting of the artist, his automatic-unconscious form-control.[1]

If we look at the matter in this light the two principles of integrity and consonance seem to merge into a single undifferentiated principle of unity, which may be achieved in different ways—by a consciously elaborated, bounded form

---

[1] See A. Ehrenzweig, *The Psycho-Analysis of Artistic Vision and Hearing*, 1953.

(*Gestalt*), or by a pervasive texture, largely unconscious in origin.

20. We are to think of works in this class, then, as achieving their necessary integrity by roundabout means. And if the concept of integrity is stretched so far it may be asked whether there is any real meaning left in it, whether there is anything that it will not comprehend. I think there is—the radio serial that drags on for years and ends, if ever, from mere exhaustion; the adventures of Sherlock Holmes, which may be collected into an omnibus volume, but obviously fall into a number of quite separate episodes. It is rare to find the more developed kinds of literature assuming such forms; but Pound's *Cantos* seem to be approaching such a condition; and other works whose direction and principle of coherence remain uncertain have solved the problem by remaining frankly unfinished, like Byron's *Don Juan*. We have many examples, too, of inorganic additions to works that were wholes already, like the second part of *Pamela*, the further exploits of Robinson Crusoe, and *Wilhelm Meisters Wanderjahre* (if indeed the *Lehrjahre* were already a whole). We also find works of great beauty and insight that yet remain imperfect because they pose a situation or a problem and then fade out without resolving it, or give a resolution that is inorganic or contrived (*Wahlverwandtschaften, Le Grand Meaulnes*).

21. Another approach altogether to the formal consideration of literature is made by Poe.[1] Poe maintains that the long poem does not exist, that all long poems fall apart into a number of short poems. He asserts strongly the principle of

[1] In his essays 'The Poetic Principle' and 'The Philosophy of Composition'.

unity (which we have called integrity), but says that it can only subsist in works of such a length as to be grasped in a single sitting. He was evidently not able to sit for long; this length later turns out to be about a hundred lines. In fact he denies the possibility of integrity except in a single act of apprehension. The idea of a sustained complex, structural unity is dismissed.

Here we are concerned not with a special kind of literature, but with a special way of looking at literature. It may seem a mere eccentricity, but Poe's theory has had its progeny in Imagist theory, in Pound's 'ideogrammic method', and in the idea of 'epiphanies', moments of illumination propounded by Stephen Dedalus in *Portrait of the Artist*.

I have discussed these later developments elsewhere.[1] On its first appearance in Poe this theory is an Aristotelian heresy, an exaggeration and perversion of traditional formal conceptions. Poe insists on the principle of unity; and then invokes (knowingly or unknowingly) the other Aristotelian principle of 'a certain magnitude'—that neither a very small creature nor a creature a thousand miles long could properly be called beautiful, since in neither of these cases could the order and relation of the parts be apprehended.[2] He becomes eccentric only in his idea of what the proper magnitude is. If he read Aristotle he did not read far enough. He conceives the proper magnitude as what can be grasped in a single act of apprehension: Aristotle conceives it as 'a length which can be easily embraced by the memory'. We are not to call upon authority in these matters. Poe might be right and Aristotle wrong. But surely this is not so. Literary experience is by its nature extended in time. To try to reduce it to something like instantaneous apprehension is to contradict its mode of being. 'An image is that which presents an intellectual and emotional complex in an instant of time.'[3] But to make this instantaneous act of apprehension the unit of literary expression is to conflate literature with the visual arts. To do this may stimu-

---

[1] *Image and Experience*, 1960, pp. 3–28.
[2] *Poetics*, 7.
[3] Ezra Pound, *Literary Essays*, 1954, p. 4.

late certain kinds of poetic activity (in fact it did): but poetic activity may be stimulated by a love affair, by the taste of a madeleine, by the smell of rotten apples. We may not build theories on these accidents. Criticism depends on keeping distinct things distinct; and a distinctive, irreducible feature of literature is its temporal extension. It is therefore vitally dependent on memory, and its natural unit is what Aristotle says it is—'what can be easily embraced by the memory'. And our normal literary experience of the unity-in-diversity of a long poem can be allowed to return.

22. But like many heresies, Poe's calls attention to something that is worth attending to. It is not true that a long poem falls apart into a number of short poems. But it is true that a long poem concentrates itself in certain focal points, certain centres of interest. When we stand back from a work on a considerable scale, or recall it after a lapse of time, it will be these focal points that come first to the attention. And another way of approaching the total form of such works will be to see it as something radiating out from these focal points. This in essence is the attitude of Longinus; and it is what is recommended by Wilson Knight's principles of Shakespearean interpretation.[1] Unfortunately, it is rarely exemplified by his practice; but it is a perfectly possible method.

The besetting fallacies of such a method are to suppose that the focal points are unrelated, or that the circle has no circumference. And once the relations are made clear and the circumference defined we get back to something like formal criticism of the traditional kind.

[1] *The Wheel of Fire*, 1930, chap. I.

CHAPTER FOUR

MORAL THEORY

23. Moral theory says that the law of perfection for literature is the same as the law of perfection for life. Literature is rightly ordered by the same principles as govern the rest of man's experience, and it is rightly judged by the degree to which it contributes to the fullness of human activity.

But each particular human activity is to some extent a special case, literature no less than the others. To write a work of literature is activity of a peculiar kind; to read a work of literature is experience of a peculiar kind. It is required therefore of moral theory that it shall tell us how the special case fits into the general scheme, how literature relates to the sum of human experience.

There is no single answer to this question, nor even a co-ordinate set of answers to which we can give equal status. There is rather a series of answers in an ascending scale of comprehensiveness.

24. The simplest answer is that literature is exemplary. It provides us with notable examples of virtues to be emulated and vices to be shunned. This is the way moral theory has been commonly felt and overtly expressed at most periods. And when literature is under attack its advocates tend generally to fall back on this line of defence.

Clearly it has a measure of truth. At all times men have found models of character and conduct in literature—at one time Lancelot, at another Holden Caulfield. At all times they have found warnings. But equally clearly this account of the matter is insufficient; and many propounders of the exemplary theory must have known it to be so even as they were forming it into words. With some straining it was made to work for heroic poetry: and heroic poetry was eventually written to fit the theory. That stuffed-shirt Goffredo in the *Gerusalemme Liberata* is specially tailored to this pattern. But the exemplary theory never worked well for tragedy, where painful ambivalence and divided feelings are essential to the kind. The great tragic heroes and situations offer us nothing so simple as either models or warnings. Some comedies can be conceived in this way; others equally clearly can not. And to some kinds—pastoral and lyric poetry—the exemplary theory has little application.

Moreover, there is no guarantee in literature itself that the models will be good ones, or that they will be used rightly. The *beau idéal* of one age and class, like Lancelot, may be seen by another as offering nothing but 'open manslaughter and bold bawdry'.[1] The gravest warnings may be perversely read as recommendations.

If we demand, like Plato and Tolstoy, that literature shall offer only good examples, then three-quarters of actual literature must disappear. If we demand, as Johnson appears to do in some sentences of the *Preface to Shakespeare,* that examples and warnings shall be clearly separated and exist in a state of chemical purity, the actual density and variety of literature is hopelessly falsified, and Hamlet and Falstaff will rise up to mock us.

25. If we say more prudently, as Johnson does in other parts of the same preface, that literature is like life, that examples and warnings exist in literature as they do in life, inextricably mingled and confused, we are not leaving much of the exemplary theory standing. We are merely saying that

[1] Ascham on Malory.

literature provides the raw materials for moral judgment in the same way that life does.

This is nevertheless to say something, and something that is true. Add a little to it and it becomes an important truth. Literature offers us the raw material for moral judgment and it offers us *far more* material than any one individual life can do. This is the second answer to our initial question: literature offers us an extension of our moral experience.

The moral experience of the individual is confined by his personal circumstances, his time, his nationality, his class. He can extend it, in a theoretical and abstract fashion, by a number of studies—history, anthropology, philosophy. But through literature he can in some degree actually *experience*, by imaginative identification, other modes of being. And literature is the principal way by which he can do this. That is the reason why persons of some literary culture often feel a constriction in the society of those without it. The non-literary may have an advantage in certainty and self-assurance that the literary often lack, but it is a certainty derived from ignorance of the full range of human possibilities. I take it as self-evident that the extension of the individual's moral experience is valuable.[1] 'I cannot praise a fugitive and cloistered virtue.'

26. It is likely, it has certainly often happened, that one who has thus extended his range through literature comes to discern in it, broadly rather than minutely, certain uniformities underlying the flux of human experience. These will come increasingly to be the objects of his search, and the guiding marks by which he orientates individual literary experiences. The sum of these uniformities has been given a name in traditional criticism: the name is 'Nature'. For a

[1] Though there is of course much legitimate casuistry to be done about the situation of juveniles, moral invalids, and special groups who have attained a happy and sufficient state of consciousness on a limited basis.

hundred years or so[1] explicitly, for far longer implicitly, Nature was the norm to which literature was referred. This is the third and most comprehensive principle of moral criticism. It has been formulated most compactly by Johnson: 'Nothing can please many and please long but just representations of general nature.'

Modern criticism has not made much use of this principle, to its great loss, but there has lately been an admirable restatement of it by Stuart Hampshire: 'Nature has its moral as well as its physical regularities. There is a bony structure of the sentiments and passions, which may be uncovered by one who penetrates beneath the manifest variety of feelings on the surface of consciousness. Or, in another metaphor, there are the deeper rhythms of moral life, which can be heard beneath the varying tones of different ages and of different climates. . . . The true, or philosophical, critic will therefore look to literature for a just representation of the repeating rhythm of human passion, and of the permanent types, and conditions, of conflict.'[2]

Like any principle so broad and general, this one is subject to distortion. It is easy to ascribe to 'Nature' the prejudices of a class, a time or a personal temperament. But it is one of the distinctions of a good critic that he succeeds in minimizing these distortions. Nature, that vast ambiguity, can evidently be approached in a thousand different ways. In much of what follows we shall be inspecting the approaches to Nature that criticism has most usefully employed.

[1] In England, 1660–1760, the century of neo-classicism.
[2] 'The Common Reader—a Lost Ideal', *New Statesman*, 18 Jan. 1965.

CHAPTER FIVE

MORAL THEORIES AND SOCIAL THEORIES

27. A moral theory of literature is without definite content unless it refers to a scheme of moral values existing outside it. It will be the more concrete and explicit the more concrete and explicit this scheme is. Plato again; he can tell us exactly what his moral demands on literature are, because he refers them to an explicitly formulated moral scheme. This is a great merit, even if we do not accept his moral scheme. More recent moral theories are often without definite content because they do not refer to any such scheme, only to an inexplicit bundle of moral prejudices (Leavis). Such criticism may be stimulating, but it remains arbitrary. We respond vaguely to the critic's tone, to our impression of his personality; and we have nothing else to respond to.

Literature is a social phenomenon. The creation of literature is a social act. By writing we intend to communicate; if our end were solitary contemplation, why write? To write is potentially to publish. By publishing we intend to communicate with a number of persons—a group, a class, a nation, the world at large. The values posited by a work of literature are posited as significant to a group, a class, a nation, or to everyone. Moral theories of literature are also therefore social theories.

This is not to say that all morality is social morality, or that moral judgments are social judgments. It is not to say anything about morality at all, but to say something about literature. We repeat, literature is a social activity. With one or two accidental exceptions, such as private journals never intended for publication, literature is meant to be read. What I now read was meant for me when it was written, and what was meant for me was meant for others too. Even the 'voice

30

of the poet talking to himself' is meant to be overheard; and even the most esoteric literature postulates an audience of a few kindred spirits. The badness of some juvenilia is accounted for by the fact that they are pure literary onanism, addressed to no one. The poet in a *schwere Stunde* wrestling with his own difficulties and torments, by the mere act of turning them into poetry postulates them as relevant to others.

So all literature is addressed to a group. The group may be a class in the Marxist sense—a section of society economically defined. It often is so, and that is why Marxist criticism has a genuine relevance. But the group may cut across class barriers; it may be a group that is only struggling into self-awareness. The literature of alienation from society, which comes into its strength with Baudelaire and his successors in France, seems at first to be addressed to a handful of exceptional and isolated individuals. But Baudelaire generalizes it from the start—*hypocrite lecteur, mon semblable, mon frère*. The handful has grown since then; it has become a self-conscious class, until today, for good or ill, it includes a large part of the intelligentsia of most civilized countries, the United States in particular. And part of what we mean when we describe a work of literature as significant or important is something merely quantitative—that it is related to a substantial group, not only to a small coterie.

28. We can now amend the description of moral theories given in 9. Moral theories are those that see literature as a contributory part of the activity of a social group, and value and explain it by reference to this group. But the social group is part of the social totality. A moral theory, if it pushes its analysis far enough, must value and explain literature by reference to this social totality. A moral theory will be the more concrete and explicit the more clearly defined is the social group in whose name it speaks, and it will be the more

comprehensive the more clearly and significantly this group is seen in relation to the social totality. Plato discusses literature as part of the education of the guardians—and we know exactly what kind of group the guardians are and what their rôle is to be. Literature is to address itself to a class of aristocratic rulers whose function in the social system is clearly defined. Spenser's aim in *The Faerie Queene* is to fashion a gentleman in virtuous and gentle discipline. His poem addresses itself to the class of gentlemen. But he is not quite certain what constitutes a gentleman, and their rôle in relation to non-gentlemen remains vague. Tolstoy sees literature as an instrument for bringing all men together in brotherhood; i.e. literature addresses itself to all men without distinction, to the classless society. This is why Tolstoy occupies an honoured place in Marxian aesthetics. It is also why his judgments are sometimes grotesque; for though it is sometimes given to the artist it is hardly given to the critic to speak adequately for all humanity; and his critical attempt to achieve concreteness and universality at the same time disastrously narrows the concept of art.

29. Does literature 'speak for' or 'address itself to' a group? If we say 'speaks for' we are roughly in the Marxist position. Literature is part of the superstructure that reflects the nature of the social-economic base. It would be absurd simply to deny this position; but no Marxist has been able to show how ideological superstructures 'reflect' the nature of the social-economic base; and they have almost all when pressed (beginning with Engels) had to admit the co-presence of innumerable accidental factors which modify this relation.[1] Among these factors, accidental from the pure Marxist point of view, are the deliberate choices and intentions of the writer. So it is more useful to think of the writer as 'addressing himself' to a particular class than as passively 'reflecting'

[1] Engels, letter to J. Bloch, 1890.

the interests of a particular class. This is a matter of practical utility rather than principle. It is easier to ask, with some hope of an adequate answer, whom the writer is addressing himself to (inspection of his work will generally tell us) than to ask what (uninspectable) social forces his works 'reflect'. For a brilliant use of the first question see Sartre, 'Qu'est ce que la littérature?'

The Marxist theory of literature posits a social-economic determinism and then admits exceptions which deprive it of most of its meaning. The Marxists are compelled to leave loopholes to account for the actual literary facts—accidental factors (Engels); a limited independent development of form (Plekhanov, Trotsky); or saying that poetry doesn't count (Marx, Sartre).[1] This leaves their theory self-contradictory, or else reduces it to such a loose generalization that it is of less service than it promises to be.

30. We should admit, with the Marxists, that literature is a social enterprise; but instead of saying that it 'reflects' (by some occult mechanism) a social-economic base we should say that it is addressed to a social group, and to that extent has a social meaning, whether the author is aware of it or not. We need not define the group as a class in the Marxist sense—a functional economic class. No doubt every group to which literature addresses itself is a part of a class in this sense, and this is a matter of fundamental importance. But within these classes there are sub-groups and special interests. For

[1] The relation between base and superstructure in Marxism can be argued about endlessly; but to the critic it is clear that exceptions are perpetually being made in favour of literature. This is implied even in Marx's Preface to the *Critique of Political Economy* (*Basic Writings of Marx and Engels*, Anchor Books, 1959, p. 42), and Engels's letter to Bloch (ibid., p. 397). Similar qualifications appear *passim* in Plekhanov's *Art and Social Life* (English trans. 1953; see especially p. 226); also Trotsky, *Literature and Revolution* (English trans. Ann Arbor, 1960, p. 233). We find Marx adopting an affectionately indulgent attitude to poetry (Fréville, *La littérature et l'art* (Marx, Engels), Paris, 1936, p. 161); and Sartre expressly excepts poetry from his requirement of *littérature engagé* ('Qu'est-ce que la littérature?', *Situations*, II, pp. 63–69).

literature it is generally these sub-groups that are the directly relevant units.

Lucien Goldmann in *Le dieu caché* explains Pascal by reference to the special interests of the *noblesse de robe* and their tendency towards Jansenism. But the *noblesse de robe* are something less than a class in the Marxist sense. And how many of them were Jansenists? Goldmann does not tell us and probably no one knows. The parade of Marxian exegesis breaks down unless some quantitative indications can be given.

H. G. Wells addresses himself to a sub-group of 'new men', petty bourgeois who are rising to power as the result of a technical revolution. He makes them aware of their interests and shows them their own situation and its potentialities. But such men are only an exceptional part of the petty bourgeoisie; and Wells, by reason of his personal success, also addresses the old entrenched upper bourgeoisie, with the end of driving them to accept the new sub-class and its purposes. This is a frequent motive in English literature of the early twentieth century; but the wholesale Marxist generalizations about class struggle will not account for it.

We need something smaller and more specific than the Marxist's 'class interests' to explain adequately to whom literature is addressed.

31. Yes, but we need something larger as well. For unless literature is to be regarded as sectarian propaganda we must see behind the particular group the larger, not contradictory presence of humanity itself, the community of all men, 'general nature'. Great writers can speak directly to humanity at large on rare occasions (windbags, bishops, presidents of the United States unfortunately do it all the time); but every writer of any merit must address humanity, indirectly and in some measure, via the group he is specially qualified to address.

32. What we should have learnt from Marxism is that the writer's choices and intentions are not simple. They are the result of class attitudes in the gross sense, attitudes derived from a variety of sub-classes, and yet others that are purely individual. Wells chooses to affirm his class, but also to incorporate much of the old ruling-class ethos against which his affirmation is made—and this in some highly idiosyncratic ways. To reduce all such variations, in the manner of crude Marxism, to aberrant or 'incorrect' reflections of the class situation is to equip criticism with clumsy and unworkable tools. Yet it is from the social applications of moral theory, of which Marxism is now the chief, that we have learnt to refine and strengthen our notions of the writer's purpose. We have learnt that the effect of a writer's work may be different from that which he intends, even contradictory to it. Richardson sets out to show in *Pamela* that in English society virtue is rewarded: he succeeds in showing that what is rewarded is not virtue. Balzac is legitimist and *bien-pensant* by conscious choice: yet his fiction unveils a society working by entirely different motives.[1] Henry James attaches himself to the late Victorian upper bourgeoisie and its American analogues (captors? parasites?); yet he is driven again and again to show that the ideals of this class are without content and lead only to emptiness and frustration. And such contradictions are a large part of the total meaning of these writers' works.

[1] See Engels, letter to Miss Harkness, April 1888; and Lukacs, *Studies in European Realism*.

CHAPTER SIX

A SYNTHESIS

33. Both moral and formal criticism may be separately useful. But a complete criticism must arrive at a synthesis of the two. Any form of extra-literary determinism makes this synthesis impossible. By extra-literary determinism we mean any critical theory that sees literature simply as the 'expression' or 'reflection' of pre-existent non-literary factors. Taine: literature as the resultant of *race, milieu, moment*. Sainte-Beuve: *la littérature n'est pas pour moi distincte, ou du moins séparable du reste de l'homme et de l'organisation*; what was the landscape of the writer's childhood, what were his sisters like, etc.? Marxism: literature as the reflection of the economic-social base. Such theories either neglect the formal question altogether, or treat it as an unexplained addition, or reduce it to the same determinism. In all three cases the dialectical relation between the moral and the formal side is rendered impossible.

To explain the moral tenor of a work as the reflection of economic-social conditions is obviously possible, and in simple cases even inviting. To explain form in the same way is always inadequate. Certain gross correlations can be made; but the variety and subtlety of formal organization far surpasses any possibility of relating it to previous non-literary events, in the life of the author or the state of society. The result of such attempts is extreme crudity, or explanation that does not explain, e.g. in the eighteenth century 'the bourgeoisie continues to ally itself with the agricultural capitalist . . . in order to maintain the laws and restrictions which will keep down the price of labour. . . . Poetry reflects a belief in the rightness and permanence of forms and restrictions, [it] becomes Augustan, idealises style, measure, polish', etc.[1] The

[1] Christopher Caudwell, *Illusion and Reality*, 1946, p. 119.

crude Marxian approach generates only a textbook platitude. It is chiefly to heterodox Marxists working on the fringes of their dogmatism (Sartre, Goldmann) that we can look for more enlightenment.[1]

34. For the synthesis to be possible literature must be regarded as a project, involving both moral and formal activity. A complete criticism may start from either the moral or the formal point of view.

Criticism that starts from the moral point of view will see form as the means to a moral and social end—but as a means which also modifies the end. *The Faerie Queene* has a clear moral and social end: 'to fashion a gentleman in virtuous and gentle discipline': and it would be entirely reasonable to start a critique of the poem from this point. Spenser chooses certain formal means to this end: the structure, somewhat modified, of the Italian romantic epic. And this changes the nature of the end—the character of the gentleman and the nature of the virtuous discipline. Both become more multiform, more tolerant, more accommodating to freckled human nature than seems at first to have been intended.

Criticism that starts from the formal point of view will see the moral and social content of a work as the necessary material embodiment of a formal purpose, the means to a formal end—but as a means which also modifies the end. Joyce's *Ulysses* is an intricate formal enterprise in more than one way—the imitation of the plot of the *Odyssey*, the experiment with the stream of consciousness, the stylistic virtuosities. It would be perfectly appropriate to start a critique of the work from this viewpoint. Joyce has chosen certain moral and social material to embody these formal structures —the Dublin scene, the characters of Bloom, Molly Bloom and Stephen. And this choice has profoundly affected the nature of the formal pattern: heroic plot-structures are

[1] See Roland Barthes, *Essais Critiques*, Paris, 1964, p. 252.

transposed to the plane of ironic realism; exalted or highly intellectual styles are parodied by being employed on the commonplace and sordid Dublin material.

35. The writer himself may be aware only of his moral or only of his formal purpose. He may flatly deny the existence of any other. But here the critic must take leave to know better. D. H. Lawrence impatiently rejected all concern with 'form' in his novels. Nabokov disclaimed any interest in the somewhat scabrous material of *Lolita* and alleged that it was a pure formal structure, the result of 'a love-affair with the English language'. But it would be a guileless critic who took either of them at his word.

36. Literature presents us with certain formal structures, and these structures are linguistic; they are composed of language as paintings are composed of paint. But language also signifies things, persons, actions, events, emotions, and the relations between them. This is social and moral material; and we cannot therefore give even a formal analysis of a work without considering the nature of this material. We may consider it in a merely conventional and abstract way (as say Dryden does in discussing the drama); but to give a complete account of a work, even a complete formal account, we must consider this material in its concrete actuality; for it has had its reciprocal effect on the form.

On the other hand, literature presents us with moral and social material. But this material is presented in certain formal structures. If we consider the moral-social material without considering the formal structure in which it is realized we are not really considering literature at all; we are considering history, sociology, ethics—usually in an amateur and incompetent fashion. To give a complete account of a work, even a complete moral account, we must consider its formal organization, because it has had its reciprocal effect on the moral tenor of the whole.

From whichever side we start, this interaction between moral and formal considerations is a dialectical process; and it is this process and this alone that allows us to see the work as a totality. The synthesis between moral and formal criticism must be dynamic—always in motion, back and forth, from one pole to the other.

When we have attained a first vision of the totality of the work in this way we can go back and see more significance in the formal or moral details; and so over again. (This I suppose is Dilthey's 'hermeneutic circle'.[1]) With the greatest works of literature, it is sometimes claimed, the process is virtually endless. So it is; but it should be admitted that after a certain stage of interpretation has been reached the results become repetitive and progressively more trivial—until there is a change of historical phase, and the whole has to be seen in a new context.

37. The moral and the formal are irreducibly different. The one cannot be explained in terms of the other. They are initially irrelevant to each other because they spring from entirely different impulses—the formal from the delight in rhythm and pattern, the moral from the desire for expression. But in an achieved work of art they become related, ultimately united. There is no reason why Spenser's moral intention should be fulfilled in this particular form. There is no reason why Joyce's formal intention should employ this particular material. Yet as form and material come to modify and interpenetrate each other they form a new indissoluble whole.

This seems close to what John Crowe Ransom says—that poetry consists of a rational *structure* and an irrelevant

[1] See Spitzer, *Linguistics and Literary History*, Princeton, 1948, pp. 19, 33.

texture.[1] The word 'irrelevant' is his, and it has been questioned. His formula is partly right and partly wrong. It is right in saying that *structure* and *texture* (in his sense of the words) are intrinsically independent, wrong in neglecting their subsequent interaction and the mutual modifications they effect. But it is well to get away from the cant about some mystic and essential unity between form and content. This unity is made not found.

38. The only common foundation of the moral and the formal aspects of a literary work is that they are parts of the same project.[2] If the project is alive the relation between the two sides will be one of tension. They interpenetrate each other, modify each other, and ultimately become one because there is a current of energy between them—an alternating current, if the electrical metaphor may be permitted.

Formal organization and moral-social material may appear to be in perfect harmony; but the tension is always present. It may be very low—as say in the most unambitious kind of novel (that which is nearest to reporting), where the dialogue is little stylized, there is little sense of rhythm or pattern in the plot, and the form follows passively the indications given by the moral-social material. Or in the kind of romance narrative that simply runs 'Once upon a time . . . and then . . . and then . . . and then'. Or, contrariwise, in what we are apt to call 'artificial' verse forms, triolets, rondeaux, etc., some sonnets—in which the form is tricky and intricate, but the material is so trivial or so conventional as not to put up any kind of a fight.

On the other hand the tension may be very high, as in a Henry James novel, where material that is in itself obstinate

---

[1] *The New Criticism*, Norfolk, Conn., 1941, p. 280.
[2] We can say indeed that they are products of the same mind, but the mind is not open to our inspection. We know it only through the projects it undertakes.

and demanding is subject to masterful manipulation, structural and stylistic. Or in the greater sonnets of Petrarch or Shakespeare, or in such a poem as William Empson's 'Missing Dates', where a heavy lump of painful and almost uncontrollable thought-and-feeling is worked into an intricate argumentative and prosodic form.

Sometimes appearances are misleading. In Gray's 'Elegy' the abstract vocabulary, the quiet finality of the aphoristic phrasing, the measured cadence, all seem the perfect formal vehicle for the moral-social quietism of the content. But this quietism has in part been *created* by the form; a more turbulent regret and protest has been *transformed*. Sometimes the tension between form and moral-social content is so perfectly balanced that it gives no outward indication of its presence—as in Racine's theatre, with its concealed conflict between the violence of the passions and the extreme decorum of the verse and structure.

CHAPTER SEVEN

MIMESIS I

39. We have a tolerably clear idea of what literature is (7); we should now consider its mode of existence more closely. In the general sense 'literature' can mean almost any kind of recorded discourse, from patent-medicine advertisements and the propaganda of obscure sects ('free literature on request') to works of scholarship and science. In the special sense (the one employed here) few of these are literature. To distinguish the special sense we sometimes qualify the word and say 'imaginative literature'; and much traditional criticism simply uses the word 'poetry', not confining the sense to what is written in verse.

40. The criterion for distinguishing 'literature', 'imaginative literature', or 'poetry' from other forms of discourse was rather uncertainly suggested by Aristotle: he says it is the 'mimetic quality' (*Poetics*, 1), that is to say the fictitious quality. The point is not, or ought not to be, that literature 'imitates' objects in the real world: so does scientific and historical writing. The point is that literature creates fictitious objects. Gibbon's presentation of Marcus Aurelius affirms something about events that have taken place in the real world. It says that certain things were the case. Shakespeare's presentation of Othello makes no such affirmation. Othello exists only in the play that bears his name. There is no specific external reality with which to compare him.

This truth has been only intermittently realized and at some periods has been obscured altogether. It has been stated with the most compendious clarity by Sidney: 'The poet nothing affirmeth, and therefore never lies.'

The frequent obliteration of this distinction can be excused, because there is a large twilight area and there are many doubtful cases. To these we shall return later. And the whole discussion about imitation is in a muddle from its initial formulation in Plato and Aristotle. Plato disapproves of poetry because it is 'imitation' and not the real thing. 'Poiesis' in Greek means both 'making' and 'poetry'. But the poet does not really 'make' what he presents. The artisan makes real beds, bits and bridles; the poet only makes descriptive imitations of them: i.e. the poet is only a maker in a secondary sense. Plato is concerned about this in *Rep.* X; more concerned than is necessary, it may seem to us; and he would probably not have been if poiesis had not had this dual meaning. However, we can agree that the point is established; in this sense poetry is an imitation or mimesis.

Then Aristotle, in *Poetics*, 1, proceeds to make this 'mimetic quality' the distinguishing characteristic of the fine arts (painting, music, drama, dancing, etc.). In particular he makes it the distinction between poetry ('imaginative literature') and other kinds of discourse, historical and scientific, that may look like it. But this will not do, unless we now take 'mimesis' in a different sense. For the historian 'imitates' persons and events as much as the poet; the distinction is that the objects of the historian's imitation have actually occurred, and those of the poet's have not. The 'mimetic quality' that distinguishes poetry from history is clearly not the imitative but the fictional, imaginary quality. This must surely be what Aristotle means. The distinguishing characteristic of literature is that it is fiction, not a record of fact.

Equally with the poets, the historians and certain kinds of scientists make descriptive 'imitations' of objects in the real world. Yet their imitations are of a different kind. The historian or the scientific writer makes imitations of objects that have or have had a substantial existence; and his imitations are invalidated if they do not correspond to the actuality. The poet is not tied to any such correspondence. Homer 'imitates' the shield of Achilles though no such shield has ever existed.

41. Yet the 'imitations' of the poet, though not of specific objects with a substantial historical existence, are not cut off from the real world. Shakespeare's Othello is not an 'imitation' of an actual man who has actually existed, as Gibbon's Marcus Aurelius is. But he is an imitation of a man. Achilles' shield in Homer is not an imitation of any shield that has ever existed; but it is an imitation of a shield.

So there is a sense in which the poet is a maker: he makes things that have never existed before. Yet he is also an imitator: he makes them by analogy with things that have existed.

42. Literature is significant fiction, an imaginary presentation that has nevertheless some meaningful relation with the real world.

This is not a very recondite idea, but it seems to have been difficult to hold it steadily in the mind. Reactions to it have been various. We have been told that poetry is all lies; that it expresses the profoundest truths; that the poet nothing affirmeth and therefore never lies. We have been told that poetry represents what ought to be not what has been; and we have the popular notion of 'poetic licence'—that the poet has a special permit to say things that are not strictly true. These are all attempts to define the ambiguous status of poetry; and Sidney's is by far the most luminous.

43. This dual state—free invention on the one hand and imitation on the other—is the mode of existence of literature. It has perhaps been best indicated by Baumgarten, who says that the world created by literature is a 'heterocosm', *another world*, related to the real world by analogy.

CHAPTER EIGHT

MIMESIS II

44. Literature is significant fiction. But—as dons are fond of saying to their pupils—significant of what? Or, to put the question more generally, what are the consequences of this 'heterocosmic' existence of literature?

They seem to be:

(a) An object in literature is not an imitation of an object existing in the real world; nor is it to be judged by its correspondence with any object actually existing in the real world.

(b) All objects in literature have an analogical relation to objects existing in the real world.

45. Proposition (a) seems to be contradicted by experience. Literature continually presents historical characters and events. It also presents characters and events which, though not historical, seem very firmly anchored to the real world, e.g. the novel presents imaginary characters but shows them as living in an actual place, St. Petersburg or London, at a particular period of history.

The general answer to the difficulty is this: literature may make use of historical and actual material for the purpose of its free inventions (as Aristotle says that tragedy generally prefers to stick to the historic names), but veridical 'imitation' is not characteristically its purpose. In so far as that is its purpose it ceases to be literature and becomes reporting or descriptive writing or some kind of scholarship. But there are mixed forms, and the novel is in some sense a special case, which we will discuss separately later on.

46. Proposition (b) that objects in literature have an analogical relation to objects in the real world, is not clear. What is the nature of this analogy? If objects in literature are not imitations of objects in the real world, yet in some way related to the real world, what is the nature of this relation? This is not an easy question. Let us consult the oracle of received opinion.

It has most generally been seen as a *typical* relation. Odysseus, Othello, Julien Sorel and Mr. Micawber have never existed; but each presents a certain type of man, in a typical situation. These human types and typical situations are regarded as recurrent, perennially important in real life; that is why their literary presentations continue to matter to us. Literature on this view offers us a series of instances of common or important human predicaments. This kind of relation is postulated, or at least suggested by many critical traditions, perhaps by most of them. It is in Aristotle; that is why poetry is more philosophical than history and must obey the rules of probability and necessity. Neo-classic criticism naturally follows Aristotle in this respect; but more surprisingly, so does some Romantic criticism, e.g. Coleridge: 'I accept with full faith the principle of Aristotle that poetry as poetry is essentially ideal, . . . that its apparent individualities of rank, character, and occupation, must be representative of a class; and that the persons of poetry must be clothed with generic attributes.'[1] Modern sociological criticism, especially Marxism, sees literature as providing particular exemplifications of basic social conflicts.[2] Psycho-analytic criticism sees it as giving expression to fundamental psychic constellations —the Oedipus situation, or the archetypes of the collective unconscious;[3] and the related criticism that uses anthropological or mythological concepts sees it as re-telling in diverse and specific forms a few archetypal stories.[4]

[1] *Biog. Lit.*, chap. xvii.

[2] Marx, Engels, Plekhanov, op. cit. See note to 29.

[3] Freud, *Leonardo da Vinci*; 'The Relation of the Poet to Daydreaming', *Coll. Papers*, IV; Jung, 'On the Relation of Analytical Psychology to Poetic Art', in *Contributions to Analytical Psychology*; Ernest Jones, *Hamlet* and *Oedipus*, 1949.

[4] Northrop Frye, *Anatomy of Criticism*, 1957; Joseph Campbell, *The Hero with a Thousand Faces*, 1956.

These several kinds of criticism differ in where they look for their typical characters and situations—common experience, history, sociology, mythology, unconscious fantasy; and in the formulas they use for describing the relationship—poetry presents what should happen, imitates the ideal, the general, etc.; it 'reflects' the economic realities of its time, or expresses otherwise inarticulate archetypes. They all agree however in seeing poetry as presenting particular instances of general types.

47. We need not dispute this proposition—that literature presents analogies for characters and situations that are in some sense typical. Indeed it is obviously true. We should not be reading Homer now, they would not be reading Shakespeare in Siberia, if this were not the case. The only objection to it is that pursued in isolation it resolves itself into a rather boring kind of truth—the reduction of the inexhaustible variety of literature to a limited number of basic types.

The escape from this reductive sterility is to move towards the other pole of the dialectic—that literature is free invention.

48. In one sense this is obvious. The writer of a narrative can put anything he likes into it. This is where the psychoanalytic equation of literature with dream breaks down; the writer is in control of his fantasy, the dreamer is not. The self-communings of novelists abound in instances of their choosing, for reasons that often seem arbitrary, to give their story this turn or that. The end of that very sophisticated work *The Beggar's Opera* parodies this situation. The audience is asked to choose: shall we hang Macheath or shall we have him reprieved? The mere existence of Nahum Tate's

revised ending to *King Lear* indicates that it would have been possible to let Cordelia live. And the fact that Dr. Johnson preferred it shows that the possibility is not inherently absurd.

This is freedom to choose the tragic or the comic ending, to turn the work into the rite of winter or the rite of spring. There are several recorded cases where it seems to have been touch and go which conclusion was to be preferred. Dickens was uncertain whether to let Walter Gay go to the bad or to preserve him as the happy bourgeois hero. And there are two endings to *Great Expectations*. We often talk (and writers often talk) as if there were an obligation to be true to an archetypal situation; but it looks as though the writer is free to choose the archetype of which his work is to be the analogical embodiment even after the work has been begun. It looks even as though he is free to alter it at the last moment.

(To be sure, we can say he has made a wrong choice; that the end of his work is not what was implied at the beginning. But this is not to say that his imitation is inaccurate; it is to say that the principle of consonantia has been infringed.)

49. And there is another kind of freedom involved. Let us take works that are clearly analogical embodiments of one recurrent, typical situation—tales for instance *de casibus illustrium virorum*. These constitute a universally known and well-defined class. Yet all the concrete details, the particular events, the social setting, all the formal means, remain undetermined and vary with each individual work. The result may be *Oedipus Rex* or *The Mayor of Casterbridge*.

It is by idiosyncrasy, by the particulars that are specific to itself alone that a work comes into being as a microcosm, a complete and individual whole; it is by embodying a general, an archetypal situation that it becomes related to the macrocosm, the totality of man's experience. We see here the outline of a dialectical relation within literature itself, parallel

in some sense to the dialectical relation already observed in
critical theories.

Literary works are fictions, but they are typical fictions.
They are free inventions, but they have a smack of necessity
about them, for they are necessarily connected with the
fundamental types of human experience. If literature were
entirely contingent it would be either nonsense or the record
of fact. If it were entirely necessary (the determinate expression of certain common human situations) literature would
have reduced itself to a few basic fables.

CHAPTER NINE

NON-FICTION

50. There is a comprehensive area of intellectual endeavour known to public libraries as 'non-fiction'. This includes subjects as diverse as theology, astro-physics, psycho-therapy and beekeeping. These cause no difficulty to the student of literature since they are wholly outside his province. But there are parts of 'non-fiction'—much devotional writing, some philosophy, some history, critical essays on literary and cultural themes—that have either traditionally been considered a part of literature, or have later become so.

There is for example a publication called *The Bible designed to be read as Literature*. Whatever may be thought of this enterprise it calls attention to a real problem—that which was not designed as literature can become literature. The same can occur in other fields than scripture. The sermons of Donne and Jeremy Taylor may still be read as incitements to devotion; but they are now more often read by persons who find in them a purely aesthetic and imaginative satisfaction. Hobbes and Burke are still read as political philosophers; but at least as often by those who are interested in the wit or the rhetoric rather than in the philosophy of counter-revolution. And Gibbon's *Decline and Fall* lives on as literature though it has doubtless been superseded as history.

51. We have defined literature as fiction; but such works as these are not fiction. They were written as records of fact, as exhortations to certain kinds of conduct; as suasions to consider the state in certain ways. They were written outside

the great parenthesis within which literature occurs; but a later age has decided to displace them and put them inside.

With essays on the arts and cultural themes there has often been an uncertainty from the beginning. Pater looks like literature; Ruskin looks like art-history—when he does not look like economics or sermonizing. Yet part of Pater's aim was expository and informative; and Ruskin's instructional and practical aims were constantly being swamped by the desire to write autonomous prose-poetry.

52. So far as this is a mere demarcation dispute it is not interesting—or interesting only to the framer of syllabuses. The literature of a period cannot be studied historically without studying some things that are not literature, and it is a question of some practical difficulty to decide how much of this is necessary or reasonable. The student of eighteenth-century literature is rightly expected to read some Locke; but this hardly makes Locke literature except in the sense that he gets into the literature programme. So for that matter do the Council of Trent and the French Revolution. Ancillary topics about which the student of literature needs to be informed cause no critical problems.

The critical problem is how to regard works which were written to furnish information or to bring about certain moral or practical results, yet are now read for their own sake as autonomous literary structures.

One solution would be to abandon the definition of literature as fiction, and include in it all writing not of a specialized or technical cast. This is the older custom; it is historically defensible, and probably for certain purposes still useful. But for criticism it has marked inconvenience. It fails to distinguish the 'mimetic' imaginary quality of the central area of literature; and it confuses the activity of the critic with that of the divine, the philosopher and the historian and demands from literary study an omnicompetence that is today impossible.

It is true that critics and literary students are often also cultural historians of one kind or another; and that they all need the assistance of general cultural history. But in principle the activity of the critic is distinct; and today, when the accumulation of research and the elaboration of methods has proceeded very far, it is usually advisable to keep it so.[1] In earlier and simpler times when knowledge was less extensive and less fragmented much valuable work was done across frontiers, or by different disciplines more or less unconsciously combined.

53. So we retain the definition of literature as fiction; but add that other forms of discourse that are not fiction may participate in the nature of literature.

This can happen in two ways:

(a) By a linguistic organization whose qualities are those of literature, or approximate to those of literature, and are capable of giving an independent satisfaction, even though the work is recognized as belonging to a non-literary category, and is read mainly for non-literary reasons. When Gibbon was read as history his work also gave an independent pleasure by its ordonnance and the character of its prose.

(b) By a linguistic organization of this kind which is strong enough to survive independently even when the original purpose of the work has been superseded or become irrelevant. Browne's *Urn Burial* has no longer any value as a treatise on archaeology, which was what it was meant to be;

---

[1] This is not an argument for any particular scheme of literary education. Literary study can be kept distinct, and other necessary knowledge provided in independent courses, as is usual in America. But literary study can still be kept distinct while other necessary knowledge is provided informally, or just vaguely assumed, within the compass of a course in English literature. This is the general practice in England. One can imagine improvements in both systems, but neither is necessarily wrong.

it survives as a meditation on mortality and transience. *The Pilgrim's Progress* is read as a kind of novel by those who have no faith whatever in its scheme of salvation.

54. But—
> Thou shalt not be a friend of those
> Who read the Bible for its prose.
>   (W. H. Auden)

It must not be said that such writers as Browne and Bunyan survive by their 'style'. They are not valued for textural qualities applied to a material that has become worthless or gone dead. The linguistic organization that constitutes *Urn Burial* and *The Pilgrim's Progress* as literature includes everything that it ever did. The archaeology and the popular Puritan moral theology are still there as much as they ever were, and they are still the core of the works in question. But they are now present as imaginative structures, as fiction, not fact. The whole work, unchanged, unfaded, has moved into a different area on the intellectual map; and that is all that has happened.

The clearest illustration is offered by the Bible itself. The belief in its detailed historicity, the arguments from miracles and prophecy have long since been abandoned; but it has not on that account become a structureless congeries of great passages, a series of sounding brasses and tinkling cymbals. Nor is it a mere Arnoldian source of spiritual inspiration, with the history and the prophecy merely jettisoned. It is a collection of ancient writings informed with a vision of human destiny. History, prophecy and miracle form the very substance of this vision. It is so comprehensive that it includes almost all literary forms within its compass, and so central to our culture that it has provided the substance of innumerable later and smaller visions. That the Bible is now 'read as literature' does not mean that anything in it can be abandoned, or that it can be reduced to a series of anthology pieces. It means that the whole structure occupies a different place in our intellectual economy.

55. It would be an overstrained aesthetic purism to say that as literature Gibbon's *Decline and Fall* would be just the same if the Roman Empire had never existed, the Bible just the same if it were not also a sacred scripture. But the existence of these works as literature is equally compatible with *any* relation to history or scientific knowledge. The works remain unaltered, though their external relations may change. The literary student cannot confine his reading of Gibbon to his irony and his antitheses. And he cannot confine his study of the Bible to the prose rhythms of the Authorized Version. But it is quite irrelevant to him to know how much of Gibbon has been disproved or amended by later research; and the whole nineteenth-century argument about the historicity of the scriptures is equally irrelevant.

56. There is still some casuistry to be done about forms which in their essence seem to have mixed intentions, partly literary and partly otherwise. The necessary allegiance of history and biography is to the facts of the case, so far as these can be ascertained. But it may be that the facts of the case are such as to compose a whole that is in itself serious, complete and of a certain magnitude. And it may be possible to record these facts in a style that brings them out with the maximum expressiveness, and that affords a satisfaction in itself. Then the historical or biographical work may become a work of literature. Such is the power of literature that when this happens we are apt to take the facts of the case for granted: e.g. we think of Boswell's *Life of Johnson* as a complete

account of Johnson's life, though substantially it is only an aspect of the later part of his career. And there are doubtless some lives and some trains of historical events that could not compose a satisfactory work of literature however they were handled.

57. Autobiography may be brought under the same head as biography; but here the material is much more malleable, being more dependent on recollection and subjective impression. An autobiography is necessarily to some degree a work of imagination, and the purely literary interest therefore becomes more easily predominant. It is probably best to take such works as *Dichtung und Wahrheit* and *Praeterita* as works of imagination in which the writer has taken his own inner life, and so much of his outer life as is useful, as his subject; and deliberately moulded it to a literary purpose. If the writer has falsified the actual material this is not a valid literary objection, unless it also shows as a failure of realization or weakness of style. The autobiographer's subject is his life as he chooses to see it.

From here we pass over imperceptibly to the autobiographical or confessional novel, where the line between *Dichtung* and *Wahrheit* becomes extremely hard to draw. For critical purposes it is fortunately unnecessary to draw it.

58. Private letters that have become part of the literary canon have done so in the same way as other works whose intention was not at first literary (53). Familiar essays, which look so much like letters, are in reality a different case: they are literary from the start. The direct address to the reader that they make use of is a convention, the fictional imitation of a direct address; and the personality revealed by, say,

Montaigne, or Charles Lamb, is a constructed fictional character, however closely it may be based on the writer's subjective feeling about himself.

The diatribes against Lamb sometimes met with in the last generation for 'exploiting his personality' are therefore quite beside the mark. If we are to object to Lamb (though I do not see why we should) it must be because the values inhering in the presented personality are unworthy, or the presentation inadequate.

Both the letter and the essay pass over easily into the novel, as we see in the case of Richardson and the essays in *The Spectator*.

59. The case of the novel is different; but there are good reasons for considering it a mixed or 'impure' form. It is clearly fiction, and has no prior intention of another kind, like history and biography. But because of its particularity in time and place it owes a considerable allegiance to social reporting and social history. It has not only to be a just representation of general nature, but also of specific facts and circumstances, in a way quite foreign to the other long narrative forms, epic and romance. The novel characteristically purports to represent the state of society at a particular time in a particular place; and part of its merit seems to be that it does this justly. Dickens may mix up two poor laws and attack specific abuses when they had really been superseded by others; but his London is London in the early years of Queen Victoria's reign; and he is committed to getting the basic physical facts and social relations right. If Balzac or Stendhal set a novel in Paris under the July monarchy they are at pains to tell us of the actual political atmosphere, the social and economic tensions of that time.

The subject is large, and requires a separate study;[1] but there is a sense in which all novels are historical novels. At

[1] See Chapter XVII below.

any rate the novel has an undefined frontier with history, and part of its characteristic merit is historical—a report on social reality.

60. The outcome of this enquiry as far as critical practice is concerned takes us back to what was said in 4—literary criticism is a distinct field of knowledge, but part of its territory is also occupied by other powers. And criticisms must come to terms with them. If the critic is treating a philosophical work as literature he cannot ignore the philosophy and concentrate on the 'style'. The philosophic vision is part of his material, and he must be philosophically competent enough to understand it. He will probably approach the philosophy by a literary avenue, and he is not of course required to pronounce on the validity of the argument.[1] It is enough for him that it exists as an object of contemplation. So with history, or religious thought or whatever it may be. The philosophy or the history or the religious doctrine may have been conceived by the writer as substantial truth; for the literary critic it has become a fiction, which he contemplates and accedes to hypothetically, as he does to the plot of a tragedy or an epic poem.

Literary critics are sometimes looked askance at for meddling with other men's specialities. Wrongly, for on many occasions they must do so. They are only open to reproach for doing it in the wrong way, and for making judgments to which their knowledge gives them no right.

The error to which literary people are most prone is that of judging ideas by their style—that is to say, judging ideas which demand their own standards of verification (historical, philosophical, etc.) simply by their literary qualities. Such people often speak as though social and political ideas that are

[1] See Basil Willey, *The Seventeenth Century Background*, 1934; *The Eighteenth Century Background*, 1940; and later works. Also George Watson's essay, 'Joseph Butler', in *The English Mind*, ed. H. S. Davies and G. Watson, Cambridge, 1964.

expressed sympathetically and with distinction carry their own guarantee of validity with them; and those that are crudely and vulgarly expressed carry their own condemnation. But this is untrue; and on that account a *purely* literary education can be dangerously misleading.

61. It has also become apparent that in attempting to delimit literature we make use of two distinctions, one qualitative and the other evaluative. We distinguish literature as a special kind of discourse—fictional or imaginary discourse; and we also say that other kinds of discourse may become literature by special merit. A historical work may become literature (irrespective of its merit as a piece of historical research) by exhibiting the qualities of integrity, consonance and radiance. But by saying this we are simply saying that it is particularly well written.

We are thus in the odd position of saying that some things are literature simply by virtue of being fiction, irrespective of whether they are good or bad; while other things, non-fiction, only become literature by being particularly good. This is awkward, but it seems nevertheless to be true. Rider Haggard belongs to literature; Herbert Spencer does not. But John Stuart Mill does, on the strength of *On Liberty* and the *Autobiography*.

An imaginative work remains an imaginative work even on a very low level; but a work of scholarship, philosophy or what not only becomes an imaginative work by exhibiting the literary qualities in an exceptionally high degree—qualities that may, strictly regarded, be irrelevant to its main purpose.

CHAPTER TEN

INTENTION AND PERSONALITY

62. In the last chapter the concept of 'intention' has made a shadowy appearance.

The question of the author's intention and its place in literary judgment has been much canvassed in recent criticism. A view that is now prominent is that of Wimsatt and Beardsley—'that the design or intention of the author is neither available nor desirable as a standard for judging the success of a literary work of art'.[1]

An older and more popular view is 'that in order to judge the poet's performance we must know what he intended'. This is stigmatized by Wimsatt and Beardsley as the Intentional Fallacy; but it is no more a fallacy than their own proposition. Each of these statements has a kind of truth, but expressed in these over-simplified forms both are misleading.

63. To deal with the easier fallacy first: 'In order to judge a poet's performance we must know what he intended.'

But clearly this is not necessary. In many, probably in most cases, we have no evidence of what the poet intended beyond that provided by the poem itself, and there can be no question of a specific externally verifiable intention.

This does not quite dispose of intention however. In judging a poem we can say 'These lines were presumably intended to produce an effect of grandeur; but they are

---

[1] 'The Intentional Fallacy' by W. K. Wimsatt and Monroe C. Beardsley; in W. K. Wimsatt, *The Verbal Icon*, New York, 1958. (Reprinted from the *Sewanee Review*, LIV, Summer, 1946.)

platitudinous and inflated, and fail to do so.' Or 'This poem aims at elegance but achieves only triviality.' In criticizing the work of a friend we can say 'I see what you meant to do, but it doesn't come off.' Part of the process of judging an unsuccessful or incompletely successful poem is a matter of surmising the intention and seeing that it is unfulfilled. With a completely successful poem all is achievement, and the question of a separately conceivable intention need not arise.

It is true that in these cases, where the 'intention' is only internally deducible from the poem itself, to use the concept of intention is only an integral part of the process of examining the poem.

64. The opposing view 'that the design or intention of the author is neither available nor desirable as a standard for judging the success of a literary work of art' is, as it stands, surely fallacious.

To say that the design or intention of the author is never available as a standard seems an absurd piece of purism. Manifestly this is not the view of the poets; for at least from the sixteenth century on they have been extremely liberal in explaining their intentions and asking to be judged by them.

It is true that they have often explained them badly, and that the announced intention often fails to account for the completed work. 'Never trust the author, trust the tale', as Lawrence said. But this does not imply 'Never take any notice of what the author has to say.' An author's statements about his own works have no absolute authority; but they are at least relevant evidence. A man's testimony to his own acts is not final; but it would be a strange trial in which nobody attempted to discover what the accused thought he was doing.

65. Spenser writes to Sir Walter Raleigh about *The Faerie Queene* 'knowing how doubtfully all Allegories may be construed. . . . I have thought good . . . to discover unto you the general intention and meaning which in the whole course thereof I have fashioned.' This is the voice of literary experience and common sense. So is Wordsworth's Preface to *Lyrical Ballads*, which has in part a similar purpose—to discover a general intention.

It would be idle to deny that the Letter to Raleigh and the Preface to *Lyrical Ballads* have in fact contributed to the judgment of the poems with which they are concerned. The idea that they ought not to do so springs from a belief that all judgment of a poem should be developed exclusively from the poem itself, 'the words on the page'. But this is a confusion: the integrity and self-sufficiency of the poem is transferred to the act of judgment. The poem is indeed an artefact, complete in itself; but the act of judging it rightly involves factors external to the poem. All literature is read within a context—a historical context in the first place. The author's intention, where he has made it known, is part of this historical context. Often he has no need to be explicit about it. The conventions of the time were sufficiently well known to be guides for readers of a later day. But they were part of the author's intention too; and they form part of the standards by which we judge the work.

66. There is one class of intention that has a particularly obvious relevance to literary judgment—the intention to write a poem of a certain kind, the intention to write in a certain genre. And this takes us outside the poem into an area of general literary intentions. *Samson Agonistes* could not be judged rightly if we did not know that Milton intended to write a tragedy modelled on classical Greek tragedy. To know this effectively we have to know about Greek tragedy, about Renaissance views on it, about Milton's relation to the

literary ideals of his time, about his own literary purposes. These are not internal to the poem but parts of an extremely verifiable intention.

A still better example is *Lycidas,* which would be almost unintelligible to a reader who did not know (or who chose to forget, like Dr. Johnson) that it was intended to be a poem in the long and elaborate tradition of the pastoral elegy.

67. The prestige of Richards's *Practical Criticism* (and its offspring in what is called the New Criticism) has led to much misunderstanding on this point. 'Practical criticism' was a method evolved by giving literary students short poems to examine without any indication of authorship or date. It was first and foremost an enquiry into actual reading habits. Later it was developed into an educational method, a kind of therapeutic reading. As a means of compelling close attention to the work itself and the processes involved in reading it, as a prophylactic against conventional and second-hand judgments, it has been extremely fruitful. But it is not the normal kind of reading. And all that was *proved* by the frequent deficiencies of Richards's guinea-pigs is, as George Watson has pointed out, 'that unhistorical reading is bad reading'.[1]

It is good training to be made sometimes to ride a horse bareback, but we normally do better with a saddle and stirrups. We normally read and judge literature with such helps as we can command, many of them implicit and taken for granted. If the author has given some additional indications besides those provided by general literary and historical knowledge there is no canon by which we can be ordered to neglect them.

[1] G. Watson, *The Literary Critics,* Pelican edn., 1962, p. 201.

68. It is apparently felt that by considering an author's intention we are illegitimately dragging in his biography to help out the poem. But there are distinctions to be made. A bad political poem does not become good because we discover that the author was really engaged in a worthy political cause and intended the poem to support it. A bad sad poem does not become a good sad poem because the author had good reasons for being sad.

There is another class of intentions however: the intention to work within a certain moral field, the intention to exploit certain formal effects. These aims usually become apparent by considering the genre and the historical ambience. But with a highly idiosyncratic author, or in a period of literary experiment, this may not be so. The author may then inform us of his intention. This information remains external to the poem: its function is to put the reader in the right frame of mind, to put him on the right track.

It may be said that the work itself ought to impose the right frame of mind, and indicate unambiguously the right track. But this is to fly in the face of actual critical experience. It is not always true that 'if the poet succeeded in doing it, then the poem itself shows what he was trying to do'.[1] New work is often misinterpreted for this very reason. It is not always easy to determine the nature and direction of a literary work; and criticism has the right to use whatever means it can find to reach this determination. Criticism has its rules, but they are not like those of dry-fly fishing, put in to make it harder.

Literary judgment is of the work, not of the author; but there is nothing to forbid us calling on the author to help us to understand his work. A sensible practical thing on this point was said by Tillyard: 'It is when a man believes that the intensive study of the isolated word has gone astray or has been brought to a standstill that he is justified in seeking guidance from biography.'[2]

[1] Wimsatt and Beardsley, op. cit., p. 4.
[2] C. S. Lewis and E. M. W. Tillyard, *The Personal Heresy*, 1939, p. 44.

69. Tillyard's observation above is from *The Personal Heresy*, a debate with C. S. Lewis, related in some ways to this question of intention. The point at issue is whether what is communicated in a literary work is the personality of the author. This elaborately courteous pillow-fight does not exactly settle anything, but by now most of the questions it raises seem to have settled themselves. There was a phase of Biblical scholarship when the Book of Jonah was supposed to have been written by Jonah; and there was a phase of literary scholarship when H. J. C. Grierson could write of 'what alone has permanent value, the poet's individuality and the art with which it is expressed'.[1] Since then we have had Eliot's argument for impersonality and the force of tradition in poetry. It is grossly overstated, but it has helped to redress the balance of a purely 'expressive' criticism. By now critics are generally agreed that the supposed speaker in a literary work can never be identified with the historic personality of the author. The poet is a man speaking to men; but he speaks by means of a fiction. All lyrics are dramatic monologues.[2] We reserve this name for cases where the distinction between speaker and author is especially obvious—'The Nymph Complains of the Death of her Fawn', or 'Fra Lippo Lippi'; but even when the occasion and the emotional content of a poem were part of the actual experience of the author, as in the 'Ode to a Nightingale', the mere act of writing a poem, of making a formal construction out of that occasion and that experience, also includes the construction of a fictional personality to be its bearer.

This is not primarily an observation about the psychology of literary creation: it is more in the nature of a rule that criticism has made for itself. It is a rule by no means obvious to the general reader, but it is not merely arbitrary, like the prohibition of intentional considerations. It is necessary to preserve the integrity of the poem as poem, to prevent its being considered as biography, which is a different thing.

[1] *The Poems of John Donne*, ed. H. J. C. Grierson, 1912, vol. II, p. vi.
[2] Wimsatt and Beardsley, op. cit., p. 5: 'Even a short lyric poem is dramatic.'

70. Nevertheless, if a writer habitually draws the material of his work from his own experience the imagined speaker so created will assume the aspect of a consistent personality. A writer who does this can hardly avoid furnishing us with a good deal of incidental biography, and a secondary interest in this biography may well be aroused. To an unanalytical reader this may seem inseparable from his interest in the poetry. But the critic has no business to be an unanalytical reader.

Many writers whose work is by no means autobiographical evolve a consistent narrator-persona to whom the reader comes to respond as he would to an actual personality. But the general reader who prefers 'Dickens' to 'Thackeray' is not in fact saying anything about these two historical persons. He is speaking of the totality of ideas, sentiments and attitudes embodied in Dickens's works as against the totality of ideas, sentiments and attitudes embodied in Thackeray's works. These may differ widely from the personality revealed by biography or acquaintance. The psychology of creation is not our business; but those whose business it is have remarked that works of art are often produced by a sort of creative persona, an 'autonomous complex', as Jung puts it, distinct from the normal personality of the artist concerned.

The tenor of unsophisticated literary opinion since the Romantic age has been largely expressive in its orientations; and the general reader is apt to think of a writer's work as 'revealing' a personality to which he responds. What he is really responding to is the work.

71. But there is no obligation on either reader or critic to confine his study to the individual work. He may choose to study a writer's whole *œuvre*, in its continuity and development. He will see each work as illuminated by the others, as part of a series which when complete becomes an intelligible whole.

Criticism of this kind becomes something like the study of an author's whole intellectual, spiritual and emotional development, so far as that has found its way into his work. As criticism, its object is the work, not the personal development of the author. But it can shade very easily into literary biography, a mixed form, partly distinct from criticism; but with its own undeniable utility. The old-fashioned life-and-works often suffers from a confusion of principles, but it need not do so. And whether it does so or not it is the kind of aid to literary study that the common reader finds most congenial.

CHAPTER ELEVEN

INTERPRETATION

72. Of all the functions of criticism the one most frequently required is interpretation. Before a work of literature can be judged, or its relation to other human activities considered, it must be rightly understood; and at all times interpretation, elucidation, explanation (whatever term is current) has formed a large part of critical activity.

In recent criticism the formal act of judgment tends to be subsumed under interpretation. And it is true that if interpretation is carried far enough it includes, by implication at least, much of the process of judgment—as much perhaps, in some cases, as the critic and the reader require. But here we wish to attend to the question of interpretation in itself.

Two different concepts of the interpretation of literature are current:

(a) That it is simply to reveal the intention of the author by removing obstacles to understanding; i.e. to explain vocabulary, idiom, and syntax, to gloss obscure allusions, to clarify arguments. It is thought that the intended meaning will then stand out clear; and the expositor's work is at an end.

(b) That a work of literature contain a latent or hidden sense that is not necessarily revealed by the simple removal of difficulties. It is the task of the critic to expound this latent meaning, which may or may not have been consciously intended by the author.

73. Method (a), exposition by the removal of difficulties, sees the critic's task as largely a matter of historical scholarship. Its aim is to recover the author's original intention, or the meaning of the work as it was understood by its contemporaries. It does not preclude the possibility that the work may have acquired further meanings for later readers; but they are regarded as adventitious. A clear example of this attitude is offered by Geoffrey Tillotson: 'To read later emotions here and there into a poem is a tedious error in criticism. . . . The original meaning of a word in a great poem is the only one worth attending to. However delightful the meaning arising out of new verbal connotations, such meaning is irrelevant to the author's poem.'[1] The proper function of criticism is the revealing of the work as a historical object. The typical instances of this kind of criticism are found in the editing and glossing of ancient works, where textual corruption, linguistic difficulties, allusions that have become obscure with the passage of time, all require to be explained. Most editorial work is of this nature; but there are also many such commentaries that are not associated with actual editions. This is sometimes called 'scholarship' and distinguished from 'criticism', both by those who think of scholarship as the superior activity and those who think of it as subordinate. But it is clearly a part of criticism like any other; and criticism of other kinds would be impossible without it.

Much of the activity of this kind of criticism is not *directly* concerned with the work itself, but with extra-literary information, or with related texts which can throw light on the meaning.

Method (b), the drawing out of latent meanings, either frankly relies on the prior existence of (a) or takes it for granted. But it tends to make only slight use of historical scholarship, and does not rely on the idea of a recoverable intention or historical meaning. It tends instead to think of the literary work as having an autonomous life, of its existing as a reservoir of possibilities, not limited by the author's

---

[1] G. Tillotson, *Essays in Criticism and Research*, Cambridge, 1942, pp. xx–xxi.

intention or the understanding of his age. If the work has acquired additional meanings for later readers these are regarded as having been latent in it from the beginning. That an interpretation made today could not have been made by the author or his contemporaries is not regarded as an objection.

74. These two attitudes have been present from very early times, and can be seen clearly in the interpretation of Scripture. From the time of the Alexandrian fathers to the fifteenth century Scripture was interpreted according to the *literal* and the *spiritual* sense. (Or rather, *spiritual senses*; it is noteworthy that there is one literal but more than one spiritual sense.) Due homage was paid to both; but in fact nearly all commentators tend strongly in one or the other direction; they are literalists or allegorists.[1]

A literalist: Hugh of St. Victor. 'Let us rather choose, from the great multitude of patristic explanations . . . that which seems to have been certainly intended by the author.'[2] 'Miror qua fronte quidam allegoriarum se doctores jactitant, qui ipsam adhuc primam litterae significationem ignorant. . . . Quomodo ergo Scripturam legitis et litteram non legitis? Si enim littera tollitur, Scriptura quid est?'[3]

An allegorist: Rabanus Maurus. 'Peu importe, pense Raban Maur, que l'on ne parvienne pas à saisir le sens voulu de l'écrivain, car on a toujours un sens prévu par l'Esprit Saint.'[4] 'Nam in principio cavendum est, ne figuratam locutionem ad litteram accipias. Ad hoc enim pertinet quod ait Apostolus, Littera occidit, spiritus autem vivificat (II Cor. iii).'[5]

---

[1] See Beryl Smalley, *The Study of the Bible in the Middle Ages*, 2nd edn., Oxford, 1952; and C. Spicq, *Esquisse d'une Histoire de l'exegese Latin au moyen âge*, Paris, 1944.

[2] Smalley, p. 95; PL. CLXXVI, 808.   [3] PL. CLXXV, 13.

[4] Spicq, p. 21; PL. CVII, 391–2.   [5] PL. CVII, 389.

.   .   .

75. It may be said that the Scriptures are a special case since they are supposed to be divinely inspired, and that similar considerations cannot apply to secular literature. This is indeed said by St. Thomas Aquinas: 'God is the principal author of holy Scripture. Human writers express their meaning by words; but God can also express his meaning by "things", that is by historical happenings. The literal sense of Scripture, therefore, is what the human author expressed by his words; the spiritual sense is what the divine author expressed by the events which the human author related. Since the Bible is the only book that has both a divine and a human authorship, only the Bible can have both a literal and a spiritual sense.'[1]

In fact there is a persistent tendency to take secular literature as though it were a kind of Scripture. Homer was allegorized from pre-Socratic times; Dante (letter to Can Grande) ascribes to his work the three spiritual senses as well as the literal one; Ovid and Virgil were allegorized in the Middle Ages, and Virgil continued to be in the Renaissance; Renaissance epics were read as allegories. The corollary to the idea expressed in Matthew Arnold's theological writing, that Scripture is a kind of poetry, is the idea expressed in his criticism, that poetry is a kind of Scripture. The notion of an omnipresent inspiration pervading the whole of Shakespeare's work is covertly active in most Shakespearean criticism. Few writers can be found to say that *All's Well* is simply a bad play; most seek instead for a concealed meaning in it compatible with the meanings expressed in the greatest of Shakespeare's work. And the laborious minutiae of modern textual criticism could hardly be justified unless the Shakespearean corpus were secretly regarded as a literally inspired sacred text. Quasi-magical explanations, such as number symbolism,[2] occult meanings in proper names,[3] both em-

[1] Smalley, p. 300, paraphrasing *Summ. Theol.*, i, q. 1, a. 10, and *Quodlibet*, viia, 14–16.

[2] Spicq, p. 70; A. Fowler, *Spenser and the Numbers of Time*, 1964.

[3] Spicq, pp. 236–41; Ruskin, *Works*, ed. Cook and Wedderburn, XVII, 223, 257. (Attacked by Arnold in 'Literary Influence of Academies'); Ian Watt, *The Rise of the Novel*, 1957, pp. 18–21.

ployed in the interpretation of Scripture, reappear (admittedly as eccentricities) in the interpretation of literature. Northrop Frye sees all fictional literature as displaced myth, i.e. as containing implicit mythical archetypes of which the author and most of his readers may be quite unaware. And Ruskin sees an esoteric sense in all great literature, although he thinks of it as intended by the author.[1]

76. It is to be noted that it is not the works which are obviously enigmas or puzzles that are most commonly felt to abound in allegorical senses. Many of Donne's poems are so manifestly witty riddles that when the riddle has been solved it can be felt with some confidence that the single possible meaning has been reached. What has been concealed with such ingenuity can hardly be used to conceal something else. So a critic like Helen Gardner, much of whose work has been in commentary on Donne, inclines, in consequence, decidedly towards method (a), learned, straightforward, historical commentary.[2]

It is in Shakespeare, where generations of plain readers and playgoers have felt (rightly or wrongly) assured of the plain sense, that the philosophical critic has found an inexhaustible well of latent meanings.

77. Method (a) is easily recognized as the ordinary procedure of rational scholarship. Method (b) looks more

[1] Ruskin, *Works*, XVII, 208. 'It is a strange habit of wise humanity to speak in enigmas only, so that the highest truths and usefullest laws must be hunted for through the whole picture-galleries of dreams, which to the vulgar seem dreams only. Thus Homer, the Greek tragedians, Plato, Dante, Chaucer, Shakespeare and Goethe, have hidden all that is chiefly serviceable in their works, and in all the various literature that they absorbed and re-embodied, under types which have rendered it quite useless to the multitude.'

[2] See Helen Gardner, *The Business of Criticism*, Oxford, 1959.

dubious. The exclusive adherents of method (a) will condemn the vagaries of method (b) as irresponsibility or superstition. But method (b) is so persistent that we should endeavour to find a rational foundation for it if we can. If there is one it is this: the fact of organizing discourse into an aesthetic form raises it to a new dimension. It is no longer bound by the intentions of its author or the circumstances of its time; its existence as an aesthetic object gives it an infinite, or at least an undefined, capacity of meaning. The formal organization of literature is a partly unconscious process; and the personal unconscious of the author is linked with the collective unconscious—the innate predispositions and tendencies of the human race. This vast ocean of possibilities is indeed canalized by the occasion and conscious intention of the individual work, but we cannot determine with certainty what will flow through the channel. The work of art is a gateway to an immense flood of human tendencies, aspirations, forms and dreams. This must not be regarded as a static repository, but as a collectivity of forces which will find expression when they can. Meaning unforeseen by the author may appear because it was *prévu par l'Esprit Saint*[1]—for in this secularized context it is the collective unconscious, the mind of the race, that takes the place occupied by the Holy Spirit in the interpretation of Scripture.

78. This is a Jungian formulation that will not be acceptable to everyone. But those who do not accept it will find that similar possibilities are admitted by thinkers of a very different cast. Latent meanings springing from the unconscious are also postulated by Freudians. They differ here from Jungians chiefly in terminology and their conception of the nature of the contents revealed. Marxists find meaning in works of literature that goes beyond the author's intention and is sometimes contrary to it; the source being the social and

[1] See 74, above.

economic forces that for them are the foundations of organized human life. These forces play the role taken in other philosophies by the Holy Spirit or the collective unconscious.

An approach to the problem may also be made on linguistic lines. Those who reject the idea of the collective unconscious, or of the unconscious in any sense, may be satisfied with the idea of language as an immense reservoir of meanings. Even the simplest denotative statement contains within itself a large attendant train of connotations. Highly organized discourse such as literature works largely by controlling these connotations; they are controlled of course by the context, which admits some and excludes others as irrelevant. The deliberately conceived intention of the author admits some of these connotations only; but he does in some sense know that the others exist, and he cannot, even if he would, prevent them from being partly active. It is through this mechanism that concealed meanings are discoverable in literature and can properly be said to be latent in it.

This is the approach made by William Empson in *Seven Types of Ambiguity*; and since that time widely employed in modern criticism. And if we wish to retain the idea of unconscious mental processes (as Empson does), the consideration of language retains its importance; for it is only through the linguistic mechanism outlined above that the unconscious can reveal its workings in literature.

79. In the conflict between literalists and allegorists we can either see rationality opposed to wild fancy, or imagination opposed to a narrow positivism. So far as this is merely party politics it need not interest us; but at bottom it is something more. It is an eternal see-saw between two basic and apparently permanent attitudes of the human mind. Literal and allegorical interpretations spring from two radically different ways of looking at literature, based on radically different ways of looking at the world, themselves probably based on

an irreducible psychological difference. (Jung would call it the difference between extroverts and introverts.) In extreme cases it is therefore fundamentally irreconcilable. But there are not too many extreme cases; it is frequently possible and always desirable that the two types of criticism should complement each other. The exclusive adherent of method (a) will tend to see method (b) as wantonly obscurantist. The exclusive adherent of method (b) will tend to see method (a) as a barren positivism. And nothing very sensible can be said about this, except that the best interpretative critics have managed to avoid both positivism and obscurantism.

Origen's allegorical interpretations of Scripture were described by an opponent as 'magis divinare quam explanare'. This was meant as a condemnation, but it could also be a compliment. It is possible that the best interpretative criticism does contain an element of divination—the intuitive putting together of symptoms that the positivist observer would never have remarked.

CHAPTER TWELVE

POETRY AND TRUTH

80. Critics have been troubled from the beginning about whether poetry tells the truth and in what sense it can do so. Plato's difficulty was with the uncertainty of poetry as compared with the certainty of logic and mathematics. In succeeding centuries the doubt about the veracity of poetry took many forms; but it has revived in our day in a form not unlike Plato's—as an opposition of poetry and science. The dominant solution in modern criticism has been that produced by I. A. Richards in the twenties. Discourse is divided into 'scientific' and 'emotive'—'scientific statement, where truth is ultimately a matter of verification . . . , and emotive utterance where "truth" is primarily acceptability by some attitude'.[1] Poetry belongs in the latter class. The statements of poetry are 'pseudo-statements'; and a pseudo-statement 'is a form of words which is justified entirely by its effect in releasing or organizing our impulses and attitudes'.[1] The theory has had little influence on practical criticism, Richards's or anyone else's, for the good reason, as Northrop Frye has put it, 'That in order to produce any literary meaning at all one has to ignore this dichotomy.'[2] Richards seems to have been dazzled by a crude form of the logical positivism current at the time; but there is no need to involve ourselves in this imbroglio. The objection to Richards's theory is not that its positivism shuts out the transcendental moonlight, but that it makes a shallow and inadequate use of the positivist tools. 'Emotive' is not the necessary alternative to 'scientific'; and the effect of pseudo-statements in organizing attitudes is

[1] I. A. Richards, *Science and Poetry*, 1926, chap. 6. See also *Principles of Literary Criticism*, 1929, p. 267, seq.
[2] Northrop Frye, *Fables of Identity*, New York, 1963, p. 8.

quite undemonstrable. However, the need is not to attack a view that Richards himself has probably abandoned long ago, but to find an acceptable alternative.

81. The true alternative is to be found in a view that Richards dismisses almost unexamined—'in terms of a supposed universe of discourse'.[1] All literary utterances occur within a context; and this context can best be seen in two phases, a general and a special. The general context is literature itself; the special context is the individual work concerned. All literature is fiction. (This simple truth is buried somewhere in Richards's 'scientific' and 'emotive' distinction.) All utterances in literature therefore occur within the framework of fiction—within, as it were, an immense parenthesis (Baumgarten's 'heterocosm'). But we do not solve any problems by lumping all the utterances of literature together as 'emotive'. Within the parenthesis can be found all the varieties of utterance that can be found outside it. What particular variety an individual poetic statement belongs to, and what kind of truth is to be expected of it can only be discovered by examining the special context, the field of reference within which the statement functions. This field of reference is the work in which the statement occurs—the novel, the poem, the series of poems, sometimes (as perhaps in the case of Blake) the writer's whole *œuvre*.

82. Most of the alleged difficulties about the truth of poetic statement can be overcome by realizing that literature is fiction, and by paying close attention to their context within the fiction.

[1] *Science and Poetry*, chap. 6.

This will be made clear by examples:

(a) 'Beauty is truth, truth beauty.' This has caused difficulty because in an obvious sense it is false. Beauty and truth are not in ordinary usage equivalent concepts. But there is no need either to make a philosophical enigma out of it, or to regard it as an 'emotive utterance', present only for its effect on our 'attitudes'. It is a dramatic utterance, spoken by a Grecian urn. This statement is not made by Keats in person, nor even by the imagined lyric speaker of the whole poem; it is made by the urn, and it is exactly the sort of thing you would expect a Grecian urn to say.[1] Throughout the poem the urn has been the symbol of a changeless aesthetic harmony in contrast with the precarious satisfactions of actual life. For an *objet d'art* like the urn there is no distinction between beauty and truth; its only truth is truth to its own nature—integritas, consonantia, claritas. But there is nothing particularly 'emotive' about this; and we shall find the significance of the statement by examining its context within the poem as a whole, not in some supposed adjustment in the emotions of the reader.

(b) 'My love is like a red, red rose.' Plainly we are not required to test the truth of this statement by checking it against the known facts (if there are any) about the colouring and temperament of Burns's love. The statement does not purport to have that kind of historical truth, and nobody can ever have supposed that it did. It is about a girl in a poem. It is of course 'emotive' in the sense that it expresses and communicates emotion; but that does not make it a 'pseudo-statement'. For it also describes a state of affairs; it says, by means of a simile, that certain things are the case. It says (if I may be forgiven a graceless paraphrase): 'The girl I love is fresh, blooming, beautiful, has a ruddy complexion and (because of the age-old association of the colour red with passion) arouses desire.' These are straightforward empirical

---

[1] Attention is called to the dramatic quality of these lines by Cleanth Brooks, *The Well Wrought Urn*, New York, 1947, pp. 191–2; and by M. H. Abrams, 'Belief and the Suspension of Disbelief', in *Literature and Belief*, ed. Abrams, New York, 1958, pp. 13–18. Mr. Abrams's essay is a most valuable discussion of the whole subject of belief in poetry.

statements, in principle capable of verification (of verification in this case, of course, only within the poem). If the rest of the poem went on to show that the lady in question was like St. Teresa of Avila they would be false. And there is nothing 'pseudo' about these statements except that being part of literature they are enclosed within a fictional framework. Within the fiction they are of exactly the same kind as if made biographically by an actual person in an actual love-situation, i.e. descriptive statements highly charged with feeling. It is of course essential to these statements that the description and the expression of feeling are intimately fused and combined. This is not peculiar to poetic language; the same can occur in common speech. The peculiarity of poetic language is in the intimacy and compendiousness of the fusion. That is why it is particularly disastrous in literature to attempt a dichotomy between descriptive and emotional aspects of meaning.

(c) '*E la sua volontade e nostra pace.*'[1] We must first refer the statement to its context in the crudest and simplest way, i.e. refer *sua* to its subject, which is God. 'And God's will is our peace.' And we must know that the God referred to is a being, *the* Being, of infinite power, goodness, justice and wisdom. The statement is then not an empirical statement, but rather a logical deduction.[2] Given the existence of such a being, an existence assumed and illustrated by the whole poem, the whole structure of the *Divine Comedy*, then this line expresses its logical consequences for human life and the human will. Only an obstinate incomprehension could reduce it to 'emotive utterance'.

Richards's argument seems to have been directed against those who take isolated poetic statements divorced from their context and treat them as maxims. As moral beings we are free to choose anything as maxims; as critics we should be wrong to isolate fragmentary poetic utterances and treat them in this way. But so obviously wrong that it is not

---

[1] *Paradiso*, III, 85.
[2] It is also a dramatic utterance, spoken by a blessed spirit. But since it is spoken by a blessed spirit it has the endorsement of the whole poem behind it.

necessary to erect a whole psychological-literary theory as a defence against the practice.

83. There is of course another problem involved. We know, we cannot help knowing, that the conception of God implied by this line of Dante is also Dante's belief outside the poem, that it is also the belief of his whole culture, and that the statement therefore has and is intended to have an application for us outside the poem. It is indeed from this problem that Richards's considerations started—the problem of the relation of poetry to extra-poetical belief. I cannot persuade myself that the problem is very difficult, or that it requires the collapse of all poetic statement into 'emotive utterance'. Dante's belief is part of our whole cultural tradition. A reader now may not share it, but he understands it, he is capable of imaginative participation in it. He must have made this act of imaginative participation all along, or he has not been reading the *Commedia* at all, he has merely been passing his eyes over the page. While he is reading the poem, while he is living within its world, the assent of the unbelieving reader is of the same kind as that of Dante himself, or of a reader of Dante's day, or of a Catholic Christian of today. The difference is that when he steps outside the poem he also steps outside the orbit of this belief. The Catholic Christian does not. The believer may be better instructed, and his reading may have added overtones because it also coincides with his extra-poetical beliefs; but his situation is not fundamentally different from that of the unbelieving reader who is properly qualified and properly disposed.

84. The same sort of situation occurs with poems where the belief involved is less public than Dante's. A statement that is

primarily justified by its place in the context of the poem in which it occurs also seems to be endorsed by the poet and addressed directly to the reader. This occurs less often than is supposed, and it is often mistakenly supposed to occur because we are insufficiently attentive to context. But still, it does occur; and when the reader's actual beliefs do not coincide with the poet's exhortations there is supposed to be a difficulty. The solution is the same as in the case of Dante. The reader accepts the poet's statement as a possible point of view, one of the varieties of human experience, and makes an imaginative identification with it. He reads it as the dramatic utterance of a character whom he can understand. No doubt it is easier to sympathize fully with a poet whose beliefs are close to our own; and no doubt there does come a point where the divergence becomes so absolute that it is impossible to read the poem at all. T. S. Eliot once strangely confessed that he could not read Shelley because the ideas seemed too silly. But this was at a time when he was under the sway of strong and recently acquired theological convictions. We may suspect that later it was possible for him to hold exactly the same convictions, but with more imaginative freedom. And this is the ideal situation. The best reader has the highest degree of imaginative freedom.

85. There may also come a point where the reader may decide to limit his imaginative freedom, to decline the task of attempting to sympathize with beliefs and attitudes that seem to him repulsive, or degrading, or inhuman. He may, in the teeth of M. Sartre, decide that the work of Genet is tedious filth and refuse to go further with it. Every reader has the right to make such decisions, and probably at some time or another must make them. But they are in part extra-literary decisions; and if he makes them too often and too early he can be only a very limited critic.

They are in part extra-literary decisions because they are

motivated by the psychological constitution of the individual reader—by his psychological make-up rather than his reason or his critical sense. We can as a rule sympathize with moral positions unlike our own, as long as they do not arouse ridicule or disgust. When they do, it becomes impossible. And ridicule and disgust are for the most part private affairs, almost involuntary physical reactions, not amenable to rational control. They can be brought partially under the sway of critical reason. If we hold that literature reveals the great moral regularities that underlie the diversities of human conduct we may reasonably argue that certain areas are too remote from these norms to be amenable to literary treatment. This is an argument that moral criticism may quite legitimately use. But it still retains an element of the arbitrary. No rational argument can be used to decide just where the line is to be drawn.

Or the decision may be extra-literary but entirely rational. It may be decided to limit sympathy and withdraw imaginative participation in the interests of a religion or a moral code. Again, a justifiable but non-literary decision. And disingenuous if the reasons for it are not made clear.

86. The consideration above will not satisfy those who are accustomed to look at literature as a matter of 'commitment' or 'engagement'; nor those who want an account of the effects of literature on character and conduct. I do not think we are called upon to satisfy either.

Those who think that literature demands a commitment more total and permanent than the imagined, 'dramatic' one outlined above are mistaken. It is not literature that requires this kind of allegiance, it is the ideas behind literature. As moral beings we must commit ourselves decisively and lastingly for or against certain ideas and attitudes. As readers and critics we must be prepared to entertain equally works that abet our moral convictions and works that conflict with them.

Good readers do not scribble 'very true' and 'pernicious nonsense' in the margins of volumes of poetry.

As to the effects of literature on character and conduct—the lasting effects, that is to say, of the temporary imaginative identifications made during reading—the truth is that we know very little about them. We have discussed literature as a vicarious widening and ordering of experience (25, 26). This is largely a cognitive matter; how our conative dispositions are affected remains very obscure. It would seem plausible to suppose, as Plato does, that imitations often repeated become second nature, and that the habitual imaginative entertaining of certain passions in literature will intensify similar passions in life. But this has been denied—by Aristotle in the first place and later by psycho-analytically oriented critics—and the discussion continues to the present day. The Platonists say that horror-comics will turn our children into sadists; the Aristotelians say that they provide a harmless fantasy gratification for sadistic feelings that are present anyway and might find a worse outlet.

We lack the information to decide; and though the question is obviously of great importance it is not primarily a literary one. It must be answered by the psychologist and the sociologist rather than the critic.

CHAPTER THIRTEEN

THEORY OF KINDS

87. Criticism before the Romantic period was in large part based on the theory of literary kinds—the division of literature into separate genres, each with its own province, its appropriate structure and rhetoric. Since the Romantic period this has been largely neglected, but it was a valuable element in the older criticism and we still need it.

The impetus to the theory of kinds was initially given by Aristotle, who discussed tragedy, comedy and epic as separate genres; and it was encouraged by the rhetorical division of styles into the high, the middle and the low. In neo-classical times the analysis of literature into distinct genres—tragedy, comedy, epic or heroic poetry, pastoral, satire, lyric—was firmly established.

With the development of the vernacular literatures the old genres ceased to correspond closely with the literary realities. It is only in a very peculiar sense that the *Divina Commedia* is a comedy, or the stories in Chaucer's *Monk's Tale* tragedies. But the traditional scheme retained its power, was reinvigorated at the Renaissance, and generated much theoretical criticism about the rules of tragedy, the proper recipe for making a heroic poem, etc. It also inspired much poetic practice, some good, some bad. If we want to make the worst of it we can cite Trissino's *Italia Liberata*; if we want to make the best we can cite *Paradise Lost*. But much of the best Renaissance literature grew up outside the orbit of this legislation, and by the middle of the eighteenth century, with the rise of new forms, especially of prose fiction, its inadequacy to the actual literary facts became obvious. Genre theory was associated with a sterile classicism and was tacitly dropped.

•   •   •

88. But the theory of kinds was not an empty formalism, and it had a more philosophic basis than has often been allowed to appear. Its virtues are not in those vain phantasms the abstract epic and the ideal tragedy; but in the true and necessary principle that each literary species offers its own satisfaction, operates on its own level and has its own proper procedure. It was impossible with these critical tools to blame a poem for not being something that it never set out to be.

What is more important, the traditional genres are not arbitrary or made-up classes; they do in fact offer a rough map of the main areas of human experience. This is witnessed by the fact that we can use the literary names—tragedy, comedy, pastoral, etc.—to describe non-literary phenomena, types of circumstance, patterns of events, ways of looking at the world. The theory of kinds offers us, in a rudimentary but fundamental way, a taxonomy, a natural history of literature as a whole, based on the natural history of human experience as a whole. So far as we know how to find our way about in the bewildering variety of literature it is largely due to this ancient system of classification.

89. In abstraction the theory of kinds is no more than a system of classification. It is given content and positive value by filling each of its pigeon-holes with adequate description and adequate theory. And much of this has been done, by the collaboration, largely unplanned, of generations of scholars and critics. Some portions of this Linnean schema have been very adequately filled out. Tragedy was put on a sound basis at the start by Aristotle; much of what needs to be said about the heroic poem was said by Renaissance Italian critics. Other areas remain relatively empty. It is possible to feel that the morphology of lyric poetry is still very incomplete; we have lacked until recently an adequate theory of comedy; and prose fiction as a whole was simply left out of the old classi-

fication. The critical description of the novel, and of all that is connoted by 'realism', though by now profuse in quantity, is still in a very disordered state.

It is also true that some of the traditional distinctions became in the end conventional and superficial, based on easily reproduced external features rather than on the essential nature of the types. In short, what is now needed is a revised theory of kinds.

90. This revised theory must be more complete than the old one, it must take account of the great expansion of the literary horizon since the Romantic age, and it must return to original and fundamental bases of classification instead of fixing upon mere historical accidents. Then we shall be able to give an account of our own field of literary consciousness as completely as, say, Dryden was able to do of his.

Much of this work has been done in the last twenty years by Northrop Frye, who accepts the traditional genre theory where it is satisfactory, but has made notable additions to it. His brilliant theory of comedy[1] does what the *Poetics* did for tragedy at the beginning of our literary history; his analysis of fictional modes[2] has greatly clarified our understanding of these matters; and in prose fiction in particular he has distinguished a varied group, ἀνώνυμος τυγχάνει οὖσα μέχρι τοῦ νῦν, which we had hitherto been resigned to consider simply as abortive or anomalous novels.[3]

To surviving romantic critics and to those with an exclusive predilection for certain literary areas this will seem a pedantry, a mere mania for classification. It is not. If criticism is a distinct branch of knowledge it must be able to survey and describe its own field, objectively and comprehensively. And the distinctions we have been discussing here

[1] *Anatomy of Criticism*, pp. 163–86, further developed in *A Natural Perspective*, 1965.
[2] *Anatomy*, pp. 33–52.
[3] *Anatomy*, pp. 303–15.

have a further importance, as will be seen in the next chapter (98).

91. It should be asked what sort of congruity constitutes a literary kind. We cannot now believe that the kinds are *universalia ante rem*, that there is an idea of the epic poem laid up in heaven. And it is rarely possible to find a single element common to all examples of a kind. Tragedy and the novel offer notorious examples of the failure of this sort of definition. Instead we find groups where A has certain kinships with B and C, B and C have other kinships with D, while D is linked in yet other respects with A; and so on. Literary kinds are probably best understood by Wittgenstein's notion of 'family resemblances':

'Consider for example the proceedings that we call "games". I mean board-games, card-games, ball-games, Olympic games, and so on. What is common to them all?— Don't say "There must be something common, or they would not be called games"—but *look and see* whether there is anything common to all.—For if you look at them you will not see something that is common to *all*, but similarities, relationships, and a whole series of them at that. . . .

'I can think of no better expression to characterise these similarities than "family resemblances"; for the various resemblances between the members of a family: build, features, colour of eyes, gait, temperament, etc., overlap and criss-cross in the same way.—And I shall say: "games" form a family.'[1]

So tragedies form a family. *Prometheus Bound, Oedipus Rex, The Trojan Women, Hamlet, Andromaque, The Master Builder, Tess of the D'Urbervilles* and *Death of a Salesman* are members of it. But we shall hardly find anything common to all of them.

[1] *Philosophical Investigations*, 1953, pp. 66, 67.

CHAPTER FOURTEEN

VALUE AND CRITERIA

92. We come now to the question of literary value and the criteria by which it is judged. In fact we have been dealing with it all along, and what is said here is in part summary and recapitulation.

Capricious and unsupported value judgments have been characteristic of modern criticism—unexplained apotheoses, revaluations, dislodgments, all the meaningless fluctuations of the literary stock market; and there has been a considerable unwillingness to state an intelligible set of criteria on which those judgments have been based. Various kinds of self-interest and social prejudice, the appeal of the chic, or of the non-chic, a rhetoric of nudges and insinuations, have done duty instead. This state of affairs grew wearisome in the twenties and thirties, and it has not unnaturally led to a widespread scepticism about the possibility of any generally acceptable criteria of literary value.[1] Some degree of scepticism is appropriate, and we should not expect more certainty than the matter admits; but it is not in principle impossible to discover the bases on which literary judgment really rests.

93. The sensible, practical thing was said as usual by Johnson. He said that the only test that can be applied to works of literature is 'length of duration and continuance of esteem',[2] and that it is 'by the common sense of readers uncorrupted by

---

[1] William Righter, *Logic and Criticism*, 1963; and, if I understand him correctly, Northrop Frye, *passim*.

[2] *Preface to Shakespeare.*

literary prejudice'[1] that all claim to literary honours is finally decided. This is true; for many purposes it is a sufficient truth; and it is one of which the critic often needs to be reminded. But it locates the authority for critical judgment rather than defining the grounds for it. Things do not last long and continue to be esteemed for no reason, and the common sense of readers is presumably established on some foundation.

We must enquire therefore what the ground of this *consensus gentium* is. Johnson has given us the answer to this too: 'Nothing can please many and please long but just representations of general nature.'[2]

If we take the word 'just' to include the formal considerations discussed in Chapter III[3] and the words 'general nature' to include the moral considerations discussed in Chapters IV and V we find that Johnson's proposition has already been illustrated in the central parts of the present enquiry. The principles by which the two kinds of judgment are combined have been suggested in Chapter VI. The mimetic considerations discussed in Chapters VII and VIII are also relevant, but they do not provide grounds of judgment in themselves, or only very rudimentary ones. They may enter however as an element into both moral and formal judgments. (97 below.)

94. It is easier to establish formal criteria than moral ones. The general formal criteria have been specified already—integrity, consonance, and radiance (Chapter III). These are extremely abstract, and gain specific literary content only when they are applied. A recapitulation and a few additional notes on them are given here, but their detailed application is precisely the work of the whole body of practical formal criticism.

(a) Integrity. The Aristotelian requirements for unity and

[1] *Life of Gray.*
[2] *Preface to Shakespeare.*
[3] It means 'accurate' to be sure; but I think it also means 'formally appropriate' or 'formally correct'.

completeness of plot in tragedy are often applied, by a natural and appropriate extension, to other fictional forms. But we should beware of conceiving integrity in purely Aristotelian and structural terms. We must recognize other kinds of integrity, expressly rejected by Aristotle—unity of hero, the uniting principle of the picaresque novel; and yet others that he never thought of—unity of character and temper, as in a meditative and discursive poem like Yeats's *The Tower*; or unity of emotional tone, sometimes conveyed more by sound and rhythm than by sense, as in some of Shelley's lyrics.

The importance of integrity as a criterion increases with the complexity of the material to be integrated. Small and simple forms achieve an easy unity; it is in the masterful unification of diverse, powerful and obstinate themes that the force and the necessity of integration are most plainly seen.

(b) Consonance. We must avoid assimilating this exclusively to neo-classical decorum. It can also accommodate violent clashes of tone and feeling, if they are consistent with the design and purpose of the whole. As with integrity, so with consonance: it is in a consistency imposed on resistant materials that consonance is strongest. There is no great virtue in an easy monotone. Consonance does not mean smoothness, and may appear in a rough as much as in a polished texture.

(c) Radiance. This is particularly various in its application, as we can see from the great range and subtlety of stylistic criticism. As a bare requirement it may be satisfied by a minimal stylistic adequacy, more often taken for granted than discussed. As an ideal limit it is incantation, *alchimie du verbe*; with the heights of expressive eloquence somewhere in between.

95. Moral criteria are more difficult to specify. It is possible to reduce them to one—relevance to life. This is comprehensive

but indefinite. As conceptions of life and what is important in life vary widely so will the grounds of moral judgment in literature. But there are some uniformities. Human life is bounded by birth and death; its scene is the natural world; love, hate, the desires for glory, for power and for salvation are the greatest passions in it; duty, however conceived, is the universal regulating principle. All moral criticism keeps these points of reference in sight, even when it does not specifically invoke them. Even when it is operating on the level of social comedy or simple entertainment its judgments are situated somewhere in relation to these great constants.

Moral judgments easily become social judgments, as was indicated in Chapter V; and such judgments often concern themselves with the permanence, the extent and the importance of the social groups with which the work is identified.

96. Mimetic considerations may enter into formal judgments about consonance. If a work begins by promising to operate on a certain level of mimetic verisimilitude it had better fulfil its promise, unless there is some good reason to the contrary.

Mimetic considerations may enter into moral judgments also. If a character in a work of fiction is an impossible or improbable representation of human nature, if a train of events offered as a mimesis of actuality contradicts our sense of the way things happen, our moral judgment of the whole work is affected. The instantaneous conversion and the *deus ex machina* are examples. They have their place in myth and romance; in realistic fiction they are moral short cuts and the work is devalued accordingly.

But in itself probability is not a criterion. It only becomes so in particular contexts. Half the great literature of the world is not concerned with mimetic probability at all.

97. Value judgments in literature are 'not absolute and definite, but gradual and comparative'.[1] There can be no *absolute* standard of expressive eloquence, of moral power, or of formal harmony. The critic must understand the nature and difficulty of the enterprise in question, know the heights that have been reached and the normally acceptable standard of achievement. There would be no way of valuing Charlotte M. Yonge if we had not, say, George Eliot to compare her with. And we could not be right about George Eliot without looking towards Tolstoy.

Above all the critic must know what to compare with what. The trouble with Arnold's touchstones is that they are all of the same kind, and that they merely mislead when things of other kinds are applied to them. To make right comparative judgments the critic should ideally know the whole of literature. This is obviously impossible; but what is both possible and necessary is that his knowledge, though incomplete, should extend *over the whole range* of literature.[2] It is not possible to form adequate literary judgments by being merely an expert on sixteenth-century sonnets, or having an exclusive devotion to the novels of Henry James.

98. Literary judgment is not a deductive system springing from a single root. Literature makes its connections with life at many points and by a variety of different means. Whatever 'general nature' may be for cosmology or metaphysics, for literature it is not a unified order. An adequate account of literary value must therefore be pluralist.

A monistic account of literary value either deliberately exalts a single quality (beauty, passion, music or the grand style) and places it at the top of a hierarchy; or unconsciously elevates the procedure of one kind of literature to universal

[1] Johnson again; *Preface to Shakespeare*.

[2] And, we may add, that he should be willing to use all of it. Arnold had a wide and comprehensive knowledge of literature; but he was too apt to base his judgments on only a part of it.

law. On this system most literature is seen as an attempt to become something other than itself. Fancy is failed imagination, comedies are failed tragedies, romance is failed realism, or realism is a failure to reach the ideal. We set off in pursuit of High Seriousness across that waste land, Criticism of Life; Chaucer and Burns fall by the way, and Dryden and Pope only keep going as classics of our prose.[1]

A pluralist account of value says that literature exists at all levels from the grave to the trivial, from the tragic to the farcical, from the heroic to the domestic, from the ideal to the grossly circumstantial. It depends vitally therefore on the theory of kinds; for it is only the theory of kinds that allows us to see in any systematic way that each form of literature offers its own satisfactions, has its own province, its own procedures, and its own aims, as well as its own way of interpreting the aims of literature in general.

99. It follows that the value judgments which are most generally accepted and nearest to certainty are comparative judgments within a single kind. We can say that *Middlemarch* is a better novel than *The Heir of Redclyffe*; and rational arguments based on generally agreed criteria could be brought to support the judgment. But no rational arguments could be brought to show that *Middlemarch* is or is not better than *Orlando Furioso*.

100. We can see at once that comparisons of value between works of widely different kinds are impossible, or not worth making; but it is a little difficult to see why, if general literary criteria have any validity. It is in essence because the judgment of literary value cannot be reduced to a quantitative

[1] Arnold, 'The Study of Poetry', *Essays in Crit.*, IInd ser.

matter. We cannot give Ariosto 85 per cent for beauty of texture and 3 per cent for moral seriousness, make a parallel score for George Eliot and then put them in a class-list. And I do not think we can simply say that Ariosto was not taking the test in moral seriousness.[1] No doubt all the criteria, formal and moral, apply to all works, in principle. But they apply in very different degrees to different kinds. For certain kinds certain criteria will be almost (though not quite) irrelevant. It is possible (to reduce the matter to an absurdity) to imagine a weighting of the test, in which the various criteria would be given different values for the different kinds; and the adjusted results could be compared instead of the raw scores. But this would be quite worthless. Literary judgment is a practical art and it cannot be pursued in areas where it offers no increase of literary understanding.

101. Nevertheless we do persistently tend to see differences in value between the different kinds, and this tendency need not altogether be resisted. *King Lear* could not be better than it is in its own kind; nor *The Rape of the Lock* in its own different kind. Yet we know that *Lear* is the greater work. Degree of accomplishment is not in question. In each case it is as high as it could be. The difference is of scope and purpose between the two kinds. We tend to express this difference by using the word 'great' rather than the word 'good'; and this seems to have more to do with generic differences than with individual achievements. If we said that something was a good tragedy but not a great one we should be implying that it fell short of the utmost capabilities of the kind. But we should hardly expect a pastoral to be great; and it would surely not be possible to apply the term 'great' to a fabliau.

'Great' has connotations of moral depth and weight. And we can deduce from this if we like that these qualities have a primacy among those by which literature is to be judged. But

---

[1] He has at any rate been put to it, by De Sanctis.

that is not a reason for invoking them in cases where they are only remotely applicable. And is an imperfect work of great moral depth to be preferred to a perfect work of lesser moral depth? The question is unanswerable. So we may preserve our general sense of the difference in rank between different kinds of literature, but would be unwise to try to define it too closely. This could only offer dubious answers to questions that in practice we do not need to ask. It is probably best to take the view that good works of literature are like the blessed in heaven—they occupy different ranks, but we are not to think too much about the matter; each is fulfilled in his own station and all are blessed; *disegualmente in lor letizia eguali.*

Part Two

Part Three

PROSE, VERSE AND POETRY

102. Up to now we have been inclined to use the word poetry in the extended sense, as synonymous with imaginative literature in general. But in common speech poetry is distinguished from prose; and we must now consider this distinction.

If we consult the dictionary under the article 'poetry' we find among other special senses two definitions that contradict each other.

(a) 'Any composition in verse, or what is intended as such, irrespective of whether it possesses any true poetic quality or not.'

(b) 'Thoughts, ideas, in themselves possessing some poetic quality, expressed not in verse but in prose.'[1]

If we enquire further what 'true poetic quality' is, the dictionary discreetly falls silent.

Evidently we have three terms to consider, poetry, verse and prose. Verse and prose are mutually exclusive (or can be considered so for the present); and poetry occupies an undefined area which overlaps the prose-verse distinction.

Jeremy Bentham said he knew the difference between poetry and prose because in prose the lines go to the edge of the page and in poetry they do not. Obviously he was distinguishing between *verse* and prose—besides slyly implying that any other distinction of poetry was unreal. So long as this confusion is merely semantic it does not cause much difficulty. The context is usually enough to keep us straight. However, there is a matter of substance involved. What we actually feel, and what is expressed somewhat vaguely in our common usage, is that there is a distinguishable quality of discourse,

---

[1] H. C. Wyld, *Universal Dictionary of the English Language.*

associated particularly with verse form but not exclusively confined to verse form, that we call poetry.

103. This sense of the word poetry is midway between the most extensive sense (poetry = imaginative literature) and the narrowest sense (poetry = verse). Since this sense indicates something that we feel really to exist we should try to describe it more closely. Honorific and rhetorical definitions abound (poetry is the breath and finer spirit of all knowledge, etc.), but they are not useful for our purpose. Here we slip over easily into metaphysics, epistemology or the psychology of the creative process; but we want to delimit a kind of discourse.

Prose tends to specialize in the direction of the factual, the descriptive and the analytical; and it is sometimes said that the special province of poetry is the emotional, the expression of feeling. But this will not do. The hortatory and the rhetorical, 'emotive' in purpose and strongly charged with feeling, are largely the domain of prose. No one would be tempted to describe the speeches of Demosthenes or Cicero or Burke as poetry. And poetry may be descriptive. No one would be tempted to describe the *Georgics* as prose.

Let us try again. Prose tends to point to an end beyond itself—to indicate or to describe a state of affairs (real or imagined); to exhort to, to prescribe, or to give instructions for, a course of action.

Poetry may do these things too. It is idle to deny that it does so, and attempts to make poetry exclusively autotelic, to isolate a 'pure' poetry, always break down against the facts. But though poetry does not deprive the word of transitive significance, the primary aim of poetry is not to use words transitively, but to make a structure of words on which the imagination rests. Poetry, like prose, uses words. But it does not use them in the same way. 'It can even be said that it does not *use* them at all; one would rather say that they use it.

Poets are men who refuse to *utilise* language.' For prose discourse words are useful tools, to effect a purpose; for poetry they are ends in themselves. This view is brilliantly and profoundly stated by Sartre, a writer who is commonly thought to be little sympathetic to poetry. The passage (from which the quotation above is taken) is unfortunately too long to reproduce here, but the reader must be referred to it,[1] for it defines the quality of poetry in the sense we are considering better than any other piece of criticism known to me.

104. Poetry then makes its own verbal organization in some sense an absolute, though it may do other things besides. Prose uses its verbal organization for ulterior ends—expressive, descriptive, analytical. To use the terminology in 16, poetry is that kind of discourse, whether in prose or verse, that makes *radiance* its dominant aim.

Since verbal radiance is to some degree present in all literature (16(c)), and since *verbal* radiance is present in literature alone and not in any of the other arts, it is easy for the term poetry to become extended, as we have seen, to cover imaginative literature in general. This suggests what Sartre would not, that poetry is at the centre of imaginative literature as a whole; that however unevenly it may be distributed through the whole, it is the vital essence of imaginative literature.

105. The fact that this distinction between poetry and prose is clear in principle does not mean that it is easy to draw. Nor is it important to draw it exactly. Individual cases may be felt differently by different readers; but it does not matter.

[1] 'Qu'est ce que la littérature?', *Situations*, II, 1948, pp. 63–71. Passage quoted in my translation.

Some obvious 'prose poems' come to mind—De Quincey's *Suspiria*, Maurice de Guerin's *Le Centaure* (with its sentence that so enchanted the young Matthew Arnold). And we can see places in writers as different as Sir Thomas Browne, Ruskin, Joyce, Hemingway, where the aim of verbal radiance suddenly takes over from the prevailing hortatory, descriptive, or narrative purpose, and we are in the presence of poetry:

'Yes, the newspapers were right: snow was general all over Ireland. It was falling on every part of the dark central plain, on the treeless hills, falling softly upon the bog of Allen, and further westward, softly falling into the dark mutinous Shannon waves. . . .'[1]

106. This does something to clarify common terminology, but the critical distinction arrived at is not of great importance. We do not in fact often want to distinguish between 'prose' and 'poetry' in this way; we more often want to see them working in collaboration.

There remains the distinction between prose and verse; and this is easier. Bentham was on the right track; verse is discourse divided into more or less regular formal units by a principle other than the meaning. The formal organization of prose arises directly out of its meaning; verse has a formal organization independent of its meaning.

Attempts have been made by free-verse theorists, and notably by Sir Herbert Read,[2] to see the formal organization of verse as arising directly out of its meaning. But though this way of thinking has its local applications, as a generalization about verse form it is radically mistaken. However they may come to subserve meaning, the hexameter, the Alexandrine, the English heroic line are formal structures logically anterior

---

[1] Joyce, last paragraph of 'The Dead', the last story in *Dubliners*.
[2] *Form in Modern Poetry*, 1932 and 1948. Reprinted in *The True Voice of Feeling*, 1953.

to any particular meaning that may find its way into them.

107. The distinction of verse from meaning may be seen by considering its origin. Meaning arises from the need to express, or to describe, or to persuade. Verse form arises from a delight in rhythm, that has nothing to do with expressing, describing or persuading. The delight in rhythm, first noted as natural to man by Aristotle, is also, according to Darwin, natural to animals. It can be observed in the play of small children (rhythmical bangings, cries, etc.), in the drum-beating of primitive peoples, and in the dance. It is of course physiological in origin, related to the rhythms of bodily life, of which the beat of the heart and the rhythm of breathing are the most important. The smaller rhythmical units, metrical 'feet', marked in English verse by the ictus or stress, correspond roughly to the beat of the heart. The next larger units, the individual lines of verse, correspond roughly to the rhythm of breathing.

The beating of the heart, the act of breathing, are vital movements of which we are normally unaware. To stress or reinforce them consciously by sound or movement gives an enhanced sense of life. Here we have a fundamental cause of pleasure in verse entirely independent of meaning. This independence persists. Children often delight in verse as jingle without any understanding of the meaning. Many adults on occasion do so too; and it is to be suspected those who are most sensitive to poetry are among them.

108. Rhythm as an independent source of pleasure is soon taken over for expressive purposes; but only taken over in part. An element of independence remains. Those like

Coleridge who would discover the origin of the regular rhythm of verse in emotion, or the effort to keep emotion in check,[1] are not taking their enquiry far enough back. Rhythm does become a means of expressing and controlling emotion; but it is an independent source of satisfaction first.

It is easy to see how the sense of rhythm becomes the agent of emotional expression. For obvious physical reasons rhythms faster than the normal (faster, that is, than the normal beat of the heart) suggest gaiety, activity or urgency; rhythms slower than the normal suggest melancholy, pensiveness or exhaustion. The development, the elaboration, the subtilizing, of these crude rhythmical effects form a considerable part of the technical history of verse. With the passage of time certain rhythms become conventional and acquire set forms. We then call them metres; and what began as spontaneous gesture does in the end become a matter of conscious measurement. The standard metres become paradigms within which poetry develops its meaning.

It is as well to remove the vulgar error that this formalizing of rhythmic organization has been the affair solely of grammarians and pedants. The poets themselves have been closely and technically interested in metrics. Among the English poets we may instance Spenser, Sidney, Milton, Dryden, Pope, Coleridge, Tennyson, Patmore, Hopkins, Bridges, Eliot, Pound.

The particular phonetic features used to constitute verse-rhythm vary, naturally, in different languages—quantity in Greek and Latin, stress in English and German, etc. Alliteration is part of the formal structure of Anglo-Saxon verse and pitch a part of the formal structure of Chinese verse; while in English verse both these features are expressive variables, but are no part of the formal pattern.

No more can be said here about formal prosody or the expressive value of particular rhythmic devices. These things belong not to the principles but to the practice of criticism, and to a special technical branch of it at that.

[1] *Biog. Lit.*, chap. XVIII.

109. The important matter of principle that has emerged so far is that we have two branches of literature, one (prose) with a loose formal organization arising out of meaning; the other (verse) with a much stricter formal organization independent of meaning.

We next want to ask whether this difference brings other differences in its wake. This we have partly answered already. Verse with its strict formal organization tends to attract into its sphere most poetry—most, that is to say, of the literature that makes verbal radiance its prime end. (Most but not all: 102–4 above.) The reason for this is suggested by Coleridge: the 'exact correspondent recurrence of accent and sound' that we find in verse is calculated to excite a 'perpetual and distinct attention to each part' of the discourse.[1] Discourse in verse therefore is required to be of finer verbal texture than that in prose which is read with a more general attention. And it is in part enabled to fulfil this requirement by subtleties of stress and intonation that verse alone can control.

Take Pope's line to the Goddess of Dullness: 'Light dies before thy uncreating word.' How much metaphysics and cosmology is concentrated in the single syllable un-; the whole idea of a destructive logos, the antithesis of all that has made our world. And how much of this vista is opened up by the fact that this unimpressive syllable is the subject of a metrical stress.

Close verbal criticism of poetry has in consequence always seemed natural and appropriate. Prose is taken in larger draughts; and to subject it to similar analysis has always seemed somewhat of a pedantry, or the purpose of some special kind of scholarship.

110. Until recent times, however uncertain the boundary between prose and poetry, the boundary between prose and

[1] *Biog. Lit.*, chap. XIV.

verse was clear and undisputed. Since Whitman there have been continual formal experiments of several different kinds that have tended to obscure this boundary. 'Free verse', in its numerous manifestations, is not strictly metrical in the old sense; i.e. it is not 'measured'. There have been some, though fewer, experiments in self-consciously rhythmical prose. This has led to the question whether the old prose-verse distinction is as absolute as it seemed; and to one notable attempt at obliterating it.

This is Mallarmé's essay 'Crise de vers',[1] which suggests that the real distinction is not between verse and prose but between language used with an aesthetic purpose and language used without any such intention. Verse, to this way of thinking, begins as soon as there is any conscious aesthetic organization of language. Mallarmé hails the rise of a *majestueuse idée inconsciente*, to wit, that verse is present as soon as diction is accentuated, rhythm as soon as style. This is a radical and attractive notion, and one that would effect a considerable alteration in our ordinary critical habits. It has obvious applications to the highly-wrought and specialized literature of the Symbolist movement and its aftermath. But its application to our general literary experience is less obvious. We return to the customary concepts of prose and verse simply because over most of the literary field they are more useful. And Mallarmé's *majestueuse idée* had better remain a seductive and delicate tool, used only for special purposes.

[1] *Œuvres*, Pleiade edn., p. 361. Cf. 16 (c).

CHAPTER SIXTEEN

POETIC DICTION

111. Since poetry makes verbal radiance its primary aim it has at most periods been associated with a special diction. This association has been seen in two ways—that poetry has the right to use a special diction if it wants, and that it must do so whether it wants to or not. These are really two ways of conceiving the special diction.

(a) That poetry has the right to a vocabulary of its own, to 'poetical' words that could not occur in common speech. In practice this right has generally been assumed, though its use has been much more marked at some periods than others, and in some languages than others. Aristotle devotes Chapters 21 and 22 of the *Poetics* to this poetic vocabulary. Coleridge remarks that it is more extensive in Greek and Italian than in English. In English we think especially of the aureate language of late medieval and some sixteenth-century poetry, and of the language of Gray's Odes, besides the finny tribes and irriguous vales of Augustan descriptive verse. But the phenomenon is almost universal. Gray is the most outspoken defender of this principle: 'The language of the age is never the language of poetry. . . . Our poetry has a language peculiar to itself; to which almost every one that has written, has added something by enriching it with foreign idioms and derivatives.'[1]

(b) That poetry by its very nature *requires* a special diction is in practice a largely negative canon. It means that certain parts of the common vocabulary are excluded as unpoetical. This is the general classical tradition. 'The perfection of diction is to be clear without being mean' (Aristotle). 'Words too familiar or too remote defeat the purpose of a poet'

[1] *Correspondence*, ed. Toynbee and Whibley, Oxford, 1935, I, 209.

(Johnson). And Johnson in the same passage commends a 'system of words at once refined from the grossness of domestic use, and free from the harshness of terms appropriated to particular arts.'[1]

We think of this as a classical principle, but in general it was equally observed by the Romantics. It underlies Coleridge's arguments against Wordsworth in *Biographia Literaria*; and was even observed in Wordsworth's own practice. In spite of his predilection for 'humble and rustic' speech there are no dialect words in Wordsworth, and few that would have been objected to by Johnson on any ground.

The great consensus of opinion in fact is on this side; and those who wish to maintain the contrary must remember, as Coleridge says, that 'the burden of the proof lies with the oppugners, not with the supporters of the common belief'.

112. That poetry has a special diction of its own has, then, been the general opinion of critics; and it has been borne out by the general practice of poets.

Against this we have the opinion of Wordsworth: 'There neither is nor can be any essential difference between the language of prose and metrical composition.' Most critical discussion takes the view that this is a massive piece of special pleading, adequately controverted by Coleridge. And this seems confirmed by literary history. Wordsworth is avowedly contesting the practice of the previous age; yet neither the practice of his own time nor even his own practice confirms his judgment. Within a few years of Wordsworth's manifesto Romantic poetry had evolved its own poetic diction, as distinctive and as remote from common use as that of the eighteenth century. And this seems to be a general fact of literary history, from Homer and *Beowulf* on.

Yet in the almost unexamined critical assumptions of our own day Wordsworth seems to have triumphed. Overtly

[1] *Life of Dryden.*

'poetical' language is almost universally depreciated, and what is praised is a lively and sensitive use of the vernacular idiom.

Is this a passing eccentricity, or is it a juster view of the way that poetry works? The question is perhaps hardly one of critical principle; but as it is a place where the judgment of our time seems to oppose itself to that of the ages we cannot avoid dealing with it.

113. On this there are two things to be said:

(a) The traditional view of poetic diction can never have applied to comic or satiric poetry. Aristotle and Johnson do not expressly say that they are excluding these kinds, but in fact they do exclude them. Comedy and satire make little use of a special poetic vocabulary, and do not observe the prohibition against common and familiar words.

(b) The traditional, 'classical' view of poetic diction runs counter to another principle of classical criticism—the distinction between the high, the middle and the low styles. At most times there has been some poetry in the low style that has made use of vulgar expressions and terms of art, both excluded by Johnson's canon. And the distinction of styles (which is related to the distinction of genres) is probably a sounder and more important part of classical criticism than its remarks on poetic diction.

114. There is truth on both sides, and the contradiction can be explained by the fact that the terms of this argument have been largely misconceived. The traditionalists have concentrated their attention on certain areas of poetry, central indeed, but not comprehensive. And the upholders of the vernacular and the language of common life have made

unjustifiable generalizations from their own special purposes. Let us try to look at the matter in another way.

There is first the language itself, with its total resources of expression, ranging from slang and vulgarism, through the ordinary spoken language of the day, to eloquence, learned borrowings and inventions. The literary language is a specialization of this totality; normally it excludes vulgarisms and technicalities. The poetic language is a further specialization, narrowing its range yet again in the same direction, but also widening it by employing old words, coined words and words used in special senses. But at any period the main source of life in poetic language is the actual speech of the time. Here I may quote some earlier remarks of my own:

'We realize that the living speech of the age is a constant source of vitality to poetry; but that living speech cannot be simply "fitted to metrical arrangement", as Wordsworth puts it; the life of verse springs from an ever-present but ever-varying tension between the rhythm of current speech and the formal metrical scheme. And there is a similar varying tension between the language of the age and the language of poetry. Sometimes the two come very close together; if they remain too close for too long the result is an unimaginative limitation of the themes and emotions with which poetry can deal. For we expect poetry to cope with experiences more subtle and more intense than those which "the language of the age" meets with every day. Commonly, after a time of approximation they tend to diverge; if the divergence goes too far and lasts too long the danger is that poetry develops a factitious dialect divorced from the current springs of life. Almost any statement about the relation between the two languages *may* be true, at some stage in the process. Gray's "the language of the age is never the language of poetry" was written when poetry had had a surfeit of rational discourse in a polished conversational style: Wordsworth's pronouncements when it had had a surfeit of the "cumbrous splendours" of Gray. Each was justified in its day; but to make any statement of the matter that is generally true is more complicated than either of them suspected. Perhaps we are often mistaken in trying to judge such critical pronouncements in the light of eternity—for their real function was to indicate the next thing to be done.'[1]

115. If the language of poetry, then, tends in varying degrees to become a specialization of the language of the age, we should ask on what principles this specialization is made. There are two such principles.

(a) Poetry is characteristically a learned art. It is nearly always dependent to some extent on previous poetry, and it normally expects of its readers a certain knowledge of previous poetry. This being so, the vocabulary of poetry is in part a vocabulary of allusion. Words are frequently used in poetry to recall earlier poetic usages, usages in classical and foreign tongues. This is not, as sometimes seems to be supposed, a speciality invented by T. S. Eliot; it is a consequence of the fact that the poetry of a given culture constitutes a coherent system. Allusiveness naturally becomes more marked the longer the history of poetry goes on; but in historic times it has been an almost universal feature of poetic language.

From time to time attempts are made to start afresh, and to write as though no previous poetry had ever existed. These attempts are often important and revivifying, but they occur in special circumstances and they do not last long.

So we may expect in most poetry some deformation of the current language in the direction of archaism and reference to older usages that the vernacular has lost.

Taste in this respect is particularly capricious. Ezra Pound disapproved of people who said things like 'addled mosses dank'—because, I suppose, it reminded him of Tennyson remembering Milton. Yet he himself wrote things like 'But his answer cometh as winds and as lutany', which is meant to

---

[1] G. Hough, *The Romantic Poets*, 1953, p. 77.

remind us of Provence and in fact reminds us of Ernest Dowson. There is neither sense nor profit in this fashion-magazine criticism.

(b) The form of poetry—verse form, or even the more self-consciously rhythmic forms employed in prose-poetry—is such as to enforce a close and particular attention to verbal texture for the Coleridgean reasons cited in 109. All parts of a poem, even the smallest parts, i.e. the individual words, 'must be such as to justify the perpetual and distinct attention to each part, which an exact correspondent recurrence of accent and sound are calculated to excite'.[1] This means that ideally the diction of poetry must be everywhere expressive, everywhere alive. And this omnipresent expressive vivacity will mean constant departures, small or great, from normal usage and normal diction.

A particular poet or school of poets may wish to keep these specializations of diction within very narrow limits, but they will always be present to some degree. Common speech and utilitarian prose can accommodate a good deal of neutral or inexpressive diction. Poetry cannot.

If these general principles are kept in mind most of the local arguments about poetic diction can be seen for what they are—workshop discussion about problems immediately in hand. The most interesting arguments on this subject are not matters of principle at all; they are the conversations of poets about the technicalities of their craft.

[1] *Biog. Lit.*, chap. XIV.

CHAPTER SEVENTEEN

THE NOVEL AND HISTORY

116. It has been said in several places above (40, 44 (a), 45, 59) that veridical imitation of objects in the real world is not the purpose of literature; but that there are mixed forms and that the novel is a special case. It was said in 59 that there is a sense in which all novels are historical novels, and that part of the special virtue of the novel is to be a report on social reality.

We must now consider the special case of the novel.

117. Are there any grounds for considering the novel a special case, for believing it to be related to reality in a special way? No critical theory ought to postulate anomalies unnecessarily.

But each literary kind is in some way a special case. If it were not we should not be able to distinguish it. It is precisely its relation to reality that constitutes the speciality of the novel. This is a fundamental sort of distinction, and it seems to set the novel apart from most of the traditional kinds—comedy, tragedy, heroic poetry and pastoral.

This sense of its peculiar position is intensified by its enormous predominance in modern literature. By far the greatest number of imaginative works now produced are novels. We should not on that account be tempted, as many modern readers are, to extend the standards relevant to the novel to literature in general. The novel is only one band in the whole literary spectrum.

Other kinds—tragedy, comedy, heroic poetry, pastoral—are distinguished by each dealing with a special area of human experience. The novel cannot be distinguished in this way. It covers all these areas. There can be tragic novels and comic novels. We are even inclined to speak loosely of a particular novel as 'a tragedy' or 'a comedy of manners'. We know that it is a novel all the same, and that it is constituted as a novel, not by dealing with any special area of experience, but by a special way of presenting reality.

118. The novel is a fictional prose narrative, but we need to distinguish it further. The romance is also a fictional narrative, and it may be in prose; but we feel it to be distinct from the novel. Our sense of 'the way things happen', as Henry James puts it, is not involved in the romance, which may deal in magic, or at least has characters who are in some degree emancipated from the necessities of time and space and social circumstances. In the novel the characters are subject to these necessities.[1]

The novel may include romance elements; but in so far as it does (*The Scarlet Letter, Le Grand Meaulnes*) we feel it to diverge from the central tradition of the novel.

Other forms are differently constituted. Tragedy can include a theophany or a *deus ex machina*, or be motivated by a ghost or start from a situation inherently improbable or fantastic. Comedy can have a magical or quasi-magical dénouement, and deals in impossible disguises, mistaken identities, etc. Heroic poetry has supernatural machinery, and heroes who are helped and hindered by deities and spirits. Pastoral represents a world that is confessedly visionary. The novel is obliged to represent life on the terms on which it is actually lived; its only parallel in this respect being realistic drama, which occupies a relatively small part in the total history of drama, and is largely an offshoot of the novel.

[1] The novel is distinguished from the romance in this way by Hawthorne, Preface to *The Marble Faun*; and Henry James, Preface to *The American*.

119. Not only is the novel bound by the laws of everyday probability, as no other form is, but it typically proceeds to bind itself further—to a particular time and a particular place. A novel is set in Moscow in 1812, in the Home Counties during the Napoleonic Wars, in Paris under Louis Philippe, in New York in the eighteen-nineties. And these settings are not merely incidental, because a novel has to be set somewhere; they are a vital part of the substance of the work. When Shakespeare sets his *Two Gentlemen* in Verona this commits him to nothing; there is nothing to differentiate Verona from any other place and the time is indeterminate. When Stendhal sets *Lucien Leuwen* first in Nancy, then in Paris during the July monarchy, he is committing himself to representing a verifiable external reality—the provincial nobility, then the political and official class of the capital, at a particular moment in their destiny. He is in fact committing himself to history.

The extent to which novels incorporate political and social history varies greatly, but they all do incorporate it. So all novels are in part historical novels, and part of the characteristic method of the novel is historical.

120. Are we then to judge a novel by the truth or otherwise of its historical representation? In part, yes. We certainly do so. The main reason that Scott's novels of eighteenth-century Scotland are superior to his medieval novels is that in the first he is presenting a phase of history that he knows and intimately understands, while in the second he gives us only a fancy picture. In the novels of recent Scottish history he has simply a more substantial truth to tell us. It may be said that these are overtly historical novels and so atypical. But the same considerations apply to novels of contemporary life. A large part of the superiority of *The Rainbow* to *Kangaroo* is that *The Rainbow* presents (among other things) a real stage in the social evolution of the English provinces, while *Kangaroo* is only a socio-political fantasy. The Zionist plot of *Daniel*

Deronda is of the same nature as *Kangaroo*; and its social unreality is the more marked as it lies side by side with the Gwendolen Harleth plot, of great power and authenticity.

121. We should be wrong however to judge a novel by the *amount* of social and historical reality that it incorporates. It is not a quantitative matter. The novelist is perfectly free to make his own selection from the available social and historical material, and it may be a narrow one. We do not ask in reading Jane Austen 'But where are the lower classes?' Or if we do we are foolish. Jane Austen tells the truth about a certain segment of the middle class of her time, from the viewpoint of a woman who herself belongs to that class. And it is enough. If we want to we can deduce a great deal from the presented material about social areas of which she tells us little or nothing. If we want to see how much more could have been put in we can turn to George Eliot; but George Eliot is not to be preferred on that account.

On the other hand the social and political content of a novel cannot be attenuated beyond a certain point without risk. There is no law forbidding James to present the characters in *The Golden Bowl* as living in a vacuum. But he has imperilled his success by doing so. The single remaining tap-root to social reality is the American-European imbroglio; and it is probably too slight.

122. How do we judge the historical truthfulness of a novel? In the first place we bring to bear any external information we may have; and, as Henry James suggests, we must bring to bear any information that we cannot help having. With the great novelists of the past, Balzac, Dickens, Tolstoy, this has generally been done for us, and we know pretty well, from particular researches or common consent, their relation to the historical actuality of the times they portray. But *l'exactitude*

n'est pas la verité (Matisse). Dickens can in many respects conflate the world of his youth with the world of his maturity; and
the truthfulness required of him does not suffer much. Yet the
demand for other exactitudes is absolute. He could not, for
example, be allowed to put the Bank at Hyde Park Corner.

A novelist may be allowed to invent a provincial town, but
not a capital; London must be London and Paris Paris.

He may invent a Prime Minister; but the political parties
must be substantially the ones existing at the time.

Class relations, in the superficial sense as well as in the
profounder one, must be got right. A novel set in the present
which used the class manners of a time even so recent as
1930 would seem hopelessly inauthentic.

These observations are trivial, and selected at random; but
they point to a multiplicity of threads linking the novel to
specific external realities. No other literary kind has them in
such numbers.

123. On the other hand the novel includes more of the merely
contingent, the accidental, than any other literary kind; and
this has worried some scrupulous souls.

'How to get over, how to escape from, the besotting particularity of fiction. "Roland approached the house; it has a
green door and window-blinds; and there was a scraper on
the upper step." To hell with Roland and the scraper.'[1]

'It was this particularity that disgusted Paul Valéry with
fiction. He could not induce himself to write: "The Marquise
arrived at nine", when she might equally well have been a
Comtesse, and might equally well have arrived later.'[2]

But perhaps this is not on the other hand; perhaps it is part
of the same situation as the historical specificity of the novel.
The green door and the scraper must be such as that kind of
house would have had at that particular period; perhaps nine
o'clock was the proper time to arrive at a party in the society

[1] *Letters of R. L. Stevenson*, ed. Colvin, 1900, II, 299.
[2] Robert Liddell, *Some Principles of Fiction*, 1953, p. 112; from which the
quotation above is also taken.

that this particular novel describes, or perhaps it was significantly late or early.

The novel presents a particular society at a particular time, and it is committed to presenting many things as they actually are or were; and much of its contingent detail is of a confirmatory nature, providing what James called 'density of specification'. Some of the greatest novelists (Balzac, Dickens) are particularly rich in such detail; some (Jane Austen, Henry James) largely dispense with it. But if they dispense with it they must, so far as they are successful, rely on moral particularities that conduce to the same effect.

From the formal point of view historical particulars are as contingent as the invented particulars like the green door and the scraper. There can be no reason internal to the novel that the Bank is in the City and not at Hyde Park Corner. It simply happens to be the case, and this is one of the cases that the novelist has to present as it is.

We can view the historical ties of the novel therefore in two ways. One, an honorific one, is that it reveals the movement of history in vividly realized concrete examples. The other, often seen pejoratively, is that it is shackled by a multiplicity of accidental details. But it is probable that the second is only an aspect of the first.

124. Poetry for Aristotle is more philosophical than history because history deals only with the contingent facts. The contingent facts can only become part of the universal, τὰ καθόλου, by being subjected to some degree of manipulation. Poetry is very free in its manipulation of contingent facts; the novel seems to be a sort of half-way house—partly tied to historical actuality and partly outside it.

The kind of poetry that presents large numbers of contingent facts is mostly recent, and in the light of the whole history of poetry, somewhat anomalous. Poetry in general tends to evade the specific, accidental, historic fact by periphrasis or allusiveness. *The Waste Land* and *Hugh Selwyn*

Mauberley are both (among other things) about London; they present many specific places, some historical characters, and numerous *faits divers*. They are unusual among poems in doing this; but this is the normal procedure of the novel. In Eliot's later poetry he reverts to the more usual practice of concealing or suppressing the contingent facts. The third section of *Burnt Norton* is set in the London Underground; and it has been revealed to us that the actual locale that suggested the imagery was Gloucester Road Station.[1] But this is not mentioned in the poem. In a novel it would have been, and Gloucester Road would rejoice to be Gloucester Road.

125. Any criticism of the novel which neglects its ties with historical actuality is false to the novel's real values, and empty when it should be full.

Arnold Kettle has said: '*Wuthering Heights* is about England in 1847. The people it reveals live not in a never-never land but in Yorkshire. Heathcliff was born not in the pages of Byron but in a Liverpool slum. The story of Wuthering Heights is concerned not with love in the abstract but with the passions of living people, with property-ownership, the attraction of social comfort, the arrangement of marriages, the importance of education, the validity of religion, the relations of rich and poor.'[2]

Mr. Kettle is right. And for him there is no question of history's being less philosophical than poetry; for he is a Marxist and history for him is a providential scheme. For the socialist-realist the supreme value of the novel is that it presents, with the maximum of concreteness and particularity, the forces universally at work in history. Those who do not believe that history is directed by universal forces, or do not believe that it is directed at all, must still however believe that certain limited and specific trends are observable in it, over limited periods. And even to them a large part of

[1] Hugh Kenner, *The Invisible Poet*: *T. S. Eliot*, 1960, p. 257.
[2] A. Kettle, *Introduction to the English Novel*, 1951, I, 139.

the virtue of the novel must be its revelation of historical truth.

Can we imagine a novel that was entirely false to historical and social reality and was yet a coherent and self-consistent work of art? No; if there were such a thing we should not call it a novel, but a fantasy or a romance. And we should then properly say not that it was false to reality, but that it was unrelated to any specific reality, even though it used local and historical names.

126. It must be admitted that literary critics often derive their information about historical situations almost entirely from works of fiction; and in talking about the truthfulness of such works are often therefore arguing in a circle. Are they therefore talking nonsense? Not necessarily. A truthful picture often reveals itself as such by its coherence. We know, say, from external evidence that the setting and certain circumstances of a particular novel are drawn from history. And we know at least something about the history. The novelist tells the fuller kind of historical truth that is his business by showing what kind of people must have lived in this world, what kind of motives could have been at work in it, what their consequences will be. Besides being a report on social reality the novel is a formal construction, and historical falsity in the novel will often reveal itself as internal contradiction. Mr. Verver in *The Golden Bowl* is a self-made American millionaire of a period when such a fortune as his could only have been made by ruthlessly acquisitive methods. Yet he is presented as a gentle, unworldly old man; and he has been seen by some of James's critics as a type of beneficent Providence. We can say if we like that Mr. Verver is not like any possible American millionaire of that time, and that James's fiction here, as often in his later writing, seems to be cutting itself loose from social actuality altogether. But without calling on the external resources of social history we can say (perhaps preferably) that the presentation of Mr. Verver's

character within the novel is inconsistent and self-contradictory. James does in fact show him as ruthlessly acquisitive,
from the beginning when we hear about his art-collection
(which includes a human being, the Prince), to the end, when
he is seen leading his wife away to captivity in American
City. Yet all the resources of authorial suggestion are employed to present him as a gentle unworldly old man. And the
two sides of the picture do not match.[1]

Internal inconsistencies (e.g. the invincible refinement of
Oliver Twist in spite of the surroundings in which he has
been brought up) may point to an unwillingness on the
author's part to face certain social realities. It may be enough
for the critic's purpose to point to the internal inconsistencies.
But I think we should feel that the critic too was avoiding
certain realities if he refused to go any farther than this.

127. The Marxists are right in laying stress on the function
of the novel in revealing historical reality; but they are not
exclusively right. It is the speciality of the novel to present
its characters enmeshed in social circumstances, living in history, not in an imaginary extra-historical world. But the
novel also deals with the attempts of human beings to escape
from history and social circumstances. On Marxist theory
these attempts must always fail, and novels which show them
as succeeding are not telling the truth. The Marxist critic
has to qualify his admiration of many traditional novels when
he gets to the end and finds the hero slipping through his
fingers—by living happily ever after, or being credited with
some unearned spiritual victory. He is often right. Cf.
Arnold Kettle on *The Portrait of a Lady*: 'Many besides
Isabel Archer believe that they can buy themselves out of the
crudities through the means of a high-grade consciousness
and a few thousand pounds.'[1]

[1] I am of course aware of the infinite ambiguities of this novel, and of the
difficulties of interpretation. I make these observations, true I think as far as
they go, only as an example for the purpose in hand, not as a critique of *The
Golden Bowl*.   [2] Op. cit., II, 34.

But there is a mechanical inevitability about the repetition of such judgments which suggests that they are there to enforce a doctrine rather than to do justice to the nature of the novel. Leaving aside the private opinions of novelists, critics or readers, the novel as a form quite evidently believes that human beings are to a limited degree able to free themselves from history and social circumstances. The links with historical reality are generally strongest on the setting and the minor characters, weakest on the hero and heroine. Heroes are by definition those who struggle to transcend circumstances, and in the novel they sometimes succeed, as they sometimes do in real life. The frequency of the theme of courtship in the novel is genetically a legacy from comedy and medieval romance; but it survives for another reason—because love is, for a time, a way out of history and social circumstances; and the novel chooses to make it an absolute by stopping at the moment of fulfilment. In other novels (though not generally English ones) the hero may be seeking neither social nor erotic fulfilment, but the salvation of his soul. And this is something that must start within history and the social order, but must end outside it.

128. We return to the point from which we started. All novels are historical novels; history is the field in which the novel operates. In bad novels false claims to spiritual freedom (caprice or mere wish-fulfilment) are shown as annulling history. In good novels either history remains absolute, as in realist and naturalist fiction; or history remains the ground, never denied; but an authentic spiritual freedom is presented, in flashes and glimpses, which is as far as the novel can go, transcending history and society.

Other literary kinds may explore more fully and more intensely the farthest reaches of imaginative experience. But the novel remains closest to our sublunary course. Hence its continuing power.

CHAPTER EIGHTEEN

ALLEGORY: THEME AND IMAGE

129. In a very broad sense allegory is a pervasive element in all literature. It is hardly possible to present persons or a train of events in literature without suggesting that they have some typical significance. One is almost tempted to say that this is an identifying quality of literature. We read some report of, say, treachery, sexual misadventure and violence in the newspaper, and it is there only to record the fact that such events took place. We read of the same sequence of events in a novel or a short story, and we can hardly escape the feeling that it is there to say something to us about human passions and human motives in general. From there it is only a step to seeing the characters as types of Treachery, Violence and Lust; and the tendency to see them so very easily becomes apparent in criticism. If this typifying tendency is explicit in the work we shall become aware of it as a separate layer of meaning underlying the surface narrative; and we shall say that the story seems to have an allegorical significance.

130. Commonly however we reserve the term allegory for cases where this tendency has become dominant. It then becomes the name of a literary mode in which the exploitation of these two layers of meaning becomes a formal constituent of the work. Persons, events, objects on the one hand are employed to stand for human passions, moral and metaphysical qualities on the other.

Clearly allegory is not a literary kind in its own right, for

epics, romances, dramas and prose narratives can all be allegories, and patches of allegory can occur in otherwise unalle-
gorical works. Nor is allegory confined to any particular area
of human experience: it may be an allegory of love, like the
Roman de la Rose, it may be an allegory of salvation, like *The
Pilgrim's Progress*. Allegory is a mode of presentation that
may be employed on any subject in almost any literary kind.
We normally keep the word for fairly lengthy forms, but in the
Renaissance *allegoria* was the term for a sustained metaphor
in a sonnet or a lyric poem. Wyatt's sonnet 'Whoso list to
hunt I know where is an hind' would be described as an
allegory.

Allegory has a natural basis; most mothers have at some
time given moral admonitions to their children in the form of
stories; but it is a consciously adopted mode of *presentation*
rather than a mode of *apprehension*. The mother knows quite
well the point she wants to bring home to her children, without the aid of the story. Bunyan knows quite well the scheme
of salvation apart from the train of events in which he has
embodied it.

131. Attempts have frequently been made to oppose allegory
to symbolism. It is said that allegory is a picture-writing in
which concepts and moral ideas previously known are deliberately translated into persons, objects and events; while symbolism is the realization in sensuous form of entities which
have not previously been apprehended, and cannot be apprehended except in that particular symbolic form.

'On the one hand you can start with an immaterial fact,
such as the passions you actually experience, and can then
invent *visibilia* to express them; . . . this is allegory. . . . But
there is another way of using the equivalence, which is almost
the opposite of allegory, and which I would call symbolism or
sacramentalism. If our passions, being immaterial, can be
copied by material inventions, then it is possible that our

material world in its turn is the copy of an invisible world. . . .
The attempt to read that something else through its sensible
imitation; to see the archetype in the copy, is what I mean
by symbolism or sacramentalism.'[1]

But this presents difficulties. It does not really work to
see allegory as traffic in one direction, symbolism as traffic in
the other. Most of those who have written on this subject
agree that allegory and symbolism are found together, closely
intertwined. And how are we to tell which came first, the
invisible quality or its sensuous embodiment? Error in the
first canto of *The Faerie Queene* was pretty clearly a theological concept before she was a monster. On the other hand
Arthur was certainly the British hero before he was Magnificence. But Britomart? Which came first, the vivid character or the idea of Chastity? We cannot say, and there is no
way of finding out.

132. The allegory-symbolism opposition is a false antithesis. They are to be distinguished, but not on the lines
suggested: they are not polar opposites. The opposite of
allegory is straightforward mimesis of phenomenal objects,
without ulterior meaning—what we normally if ineptly call
'realism'.

Let us use the word 'theme' for the immaterial 'abstract'
element in allegory, and the word 'image' for the 'concrete'
personages, actions or objects in which it is embodied.

At one pole we have literature in which theme is absolutely
dominant over image. The persons and events are mere con-
veniences to serve as a vehicle for preconceived thematic
material. We can call this naïve allegory, and it is always on
the verge of passing out of literature altogether. The images

[1] C. S. Lewis, *The Allegory of Love*, Oxford, 1936, p. 44. There are many
antecedents to this passage of Lewis's. The same distinction is made by Goethe,
Blake, Coleridge and Yeats. I have discussed this matter of allegory at some
length in *A Preface to the Faerie Queene*, 1962, pp. 100–38, and what I have to
say here is a re-statement of part of that argument.

are faint or incoherent, the fictional guise is too thin, and we realize that what we have is slightly flavoured moralizing. The morality plays hover about this line, sometimes landing on the right side, sometimes on the wrong.

At the other pole we have literature where image is dominant and thematic significance is minimal. The characters and events are specific, singular, non-typical. They are what they are, and suggest nothing (or as nearly as possible nothing) more general, nothing beyond themselves. We can call this realism, for want of a better word, and it too is always on the verge of passing out of literature, into reporting or non-literary informative writing.

133. Imagine these two opposites placed upon a dial, naïve allegory at twelve, realism at six o'clock. We could then move round the right-hand semi-circle of the clock-face, finding at each successive stage a decrease in the power of theme and an increase in the power of image. In the middle, at three o'clock, the two are exactly balanced. Neither theme nor image is dominant, we experience them together and feel that they are inseparable. This happens in the work of Shakespeare. Our sense of the centrality of Shakespeare comes largely from the perfect balance between image—the concretely realized individuality of his characters, and theme—their power of typifying moral and metaphysical qualities. And this balance is also found in lesser writers.

In the first quarter from twelve to three o'clock we find a gradual movement away from naïve allegory.[1] First to allegory proper, where theme is still dominant, but the images have acquired a life and interest of their own. The Castle of Alma (*F.Q.* II, ix) is naïve allegory, Redcross at the House of Holiness (*F.Q.* I, x) is allegory proper. We then come to

---

[1] The account of this sector (though not the clock-image) is taken from Northrop Frye, *Anatomy*, p. 91. Thereafter I desert him, but it was from this passage of his that my formulation started.

such things as the comedy of humours and the romance of types, where the characters no longer represent abstract qualities, but typical aspects of human nature; then to loosely ordered structures in which allegorical significance is picked up and dropped at will, like Book VI of the *Faerie Queene* or parts of *Orlando Furioso*, or parts of Ibsen's drama. Then to sustained poetic structures such as *Paradise Lost* that are no longer distinctly allegorical but have a strongly-marked doctrinal interest; and thence to the complete incarnation of theme in image that we find in Shakespeare. The sector from three to six takes us from Shakespeare's complete balance between theme and image to realism, where thematic interest is at a minimum. It is pre-eminently the field of the novel, though it also includes verse-chronicles, descriptive poetry, etc. Nearest to the Shakespearean incarnation are Tolstoy and George Eliot. Somewhere in the middle are Balzac, Dickens, Thackeray; thematic interest has not yet disappeared, but it is decidedly subordinate to the life and variety of the concrete image. And from them we pass to the deliberately objective realists and naturalists of the late nineteenth century, and the practitioners of the *nouveau roman* such as Robbe-Grillet today.

134. But the circle has another half—from six back to twelve again. Realism is a *ne plus ultra*. Any farther in the same direction takes us out of literature altogether, towards blue-books, sanitary reports, etc. So we turn inevitably towards allegory again, but by a different route and through different phases. The most important of these is symbolism, situated at nine o'clock, opposite the completely incarnate union of theme and image found in Shakespeare. In symbolism theme and image have again become completely balanced, but their equal presence is now of a different kind. In Shakespeare it is like the union of soul and body; in symbolism it is another and less familiar relation. The image, we are told, in symbolism is

the only possible embodiment of a theme otherwise inapprehensible; but this is not achieved as in incarnational writing by means of character and action—rather by means of verbal or pictorial magic. The mysterious unity of symbolist writing is achieved by evocative rhythm and sound, powerful but inexplicable metaphors, coloured vowels, *alchimie du verbe*; an attenuation of the referential quality of language in favour of 'musical' effects and rhythms that attack the unconscious; or else an attempt like that of Blake to present directly things seen in vision, with the minimum of reference to accessible human reality.[1]

Between realism and symbolism (at half-past seven) we find imagism. It can be regarded as realism with a strong aesthetic orientation. Realism is more interested in the objects it presents than in their verbal presentation, and is often associated with a certain coarseness of style. When we find writers with the same positivist, representational attitude, but also with strong verbal and stylistic interests, the stress falls less on the brute fact and more on its linguistic presentation. 'The apparition of these faces in the crowd;/Petals on a wet, black bough.'

On the other side of symbolism, in the fourth quarter at half-past ten, moving towards naïve allegory, we have what might be called hieratic symbolism or emblem—symbols become stereotyped and fixed, often visual like the attributes of saints, but sometimes literary like the descriptions of the Seven Deadly Sins in Spenser and elsewhere. Yeats with his swans and towers sometimes uses symbols in this way.

And so the circle is complete. I hope this naïve device may be forgiven; I can find no other convenient way to explain conveniently a sequence that I take to have a real importance.

135. It will be noticed that allegory proper is just away from the polar extreme, at about one o'clock. Theme is still dominant;

[1] Symbolism is discussed more fully in the next chapter.

the moral dictates the story; allegory is shaped by thematic
needs. But it is not entirely subjected to them. The images
acquire an authentic coherence and vitality of their own. In
its purest form there is a simple one-to-one correspondence
between the images and the themes that they represent; but
we do not simply look through the images to the themes; the
images themselves also arrest the imagination. Allegory is
compatible with great pictorial vividness, as in Spenser; even
with great vividness of characterization, of a 'flat' restricted
kind, as in Bunyan.

The feeling with which we started, that allegory has in
some sense a special place in the literary spectrum, has a real
justification. Allegory is the clearest instance (not the richest
and most profound, but the clearest) of the dialectic between
immaterial conception and sensuous realization of which the
life of literature is made up.

CHAPTER NINETEEN

SYMBOLISM

136. Symbolism as a literary term has no clear meaning. It is a radiant blur rather than a delimited area. However, it covers a bundle of tendencies that have powerfully affected poetry and critical thought since the middle of the last century. Among these tendencies are the assimilation of poetry to music (Poe, Verlaine, Pater); to dream (Poe, Baudelaire); to an unattainable and inexpressible ideal (Poe, Mallarmé); to magic and the occult (Rimbaud, Yeats). We find repeated assertions of the power of 'symbols' over the mind, symbols being verbal or visual presentations regarded as realizing complexes of experience otherwise inapprehensible. Sometimes this symbolic power is connected with a mysterious system of correspondences supposed to be present in Nature, as in Baudelaire's sonnet; or with the action of spiritual powers, as in Yeats. Later, with Pound and his school, the symbol is disenchanted and called an image. It is then supposed to be efficacious simply by its own configuration. Symbolist ideas are often expressed in outrageous or challenging irrational terms; but they may appear more demurely, as when Eliot regards the meaning of a poem as a mere sop to the reader's intellect, to keep it quiet while the poetry does its work on him.[1] And they may appear disguised as linguistic science, as in Owen Barfield's identification of poetic diction with a primitive, undifferentiated state of language when the object and its associations are still undistinguished;[2] perhaps in I. A. Richards's denial of referential purport to what appears in poetry as statement.

In all these manifestations there is a common thread. It is the tendency to exalt the non-discursive element in poetry; to

[1] *The Use of Poetry and the Use of Criticism*, 1933, p. 151.
[2] Owen Barfield, *Poetic Diction*, 2nd edn., 1952.

remove the language of poetry as far as possible from its referential or representational functions.

137. In a wider sense symbolism is a fundamental activity of the human mind—the power of actualizing inarticulate experience in some apprehensible sensory form. The operation of this symbolising power has been most fully analysed by Cassirer.[1] He sees it as the central, typical, universal human faculty, at work impartially in myth, religion, language, art and science, creating the human reality by giving it symbolic form. As far as art is concerned this seems in a sense obvious; what else could art be doing? But it has not in fact been the most prevalent way of looking at the matter in our culture. It has been more usual to think of art as *reproducing* experience already more or less available in other forms—to think of it in fact mimetically. Cassirer accordingly admits the prevalence of a mimetic theory up to the middle of the eighteenth century. It is then largely replaced by an expressive theory. Art does not imitate the external world, it expresses the feelings of the artist. But this is hardly more than a mimetic theory in another guise; instead of reproducing the outer world art reproduces the inner life, the life of the affections and emotions.[2] Cassirer would substitute for these the view of art as essentially *formative*. It does not reproduce pre-existing reality. There is no reality for man until he has created it in symbolic form. Art is one of the systems of symbolic form.

At bottom this is a Kantian view of art—an unreachable *Ding an sich* is apprehended only under the necessary forms given to it by human activity.

[1] Ernst Cassirer, *The Philosophy of Symbolic Form*, Berlin, 1933; English trans. New Haven, 1953. For the literary student Cassirer's thought is more easily accessible in his shorter works, *An Essay on Man*, New Haven, 1944; 2nd edn., New York, 1956; *Language and Myth*, New York, 1946; and in the work of Suzanne Langer.

[2] *Essay on Man*, 1956 edn., pp. 177–81. For the replacement of mimetic by expressive theory see also M. H. Abrams, *The Mirror and the Lamp*, New York, 1956.

'The Parthenon frieze or a Mass by Bach, Michelangelo's Sistine Chapel, or a poem of Leopardi, a sonata of Beethoven or a novel of Dostoievski are neither merely representative nor merely expressive. They are symbolic in a new and deeper sense.'[1] And symbolic, we must add, in their own way. Art is a special mode of apprehending reality, a symbolic system different from that of science and pragmatic manipulation, but equally valid and with its own rights.

138. This attitude, or something like it, has never been wholly absent from aesthetic theory, but in former times it has commonly been expressed as an honorific or hortatory supplement to an essentially mimetic way of thinking. Cassirer's massive and elaborately documented presentation of art as symbolic form amounts virtually to a new insight. Cassirer enables us to give a clearer meaning to Baumgarten's notion of art as a heterocosm, another world. Art is not a fanciful supplement to the world of science and practical activity, or to the 'truths' of religion. It is another world in the sense that it is an alternative mode of apprehending the world, one of the organs by which man creates his reality.

But we have wished in this essay to avoid general aesthetics and to narrow our consideration to the specific conditions of literary art. And the art of literature exhibits certain fundamental differences from the other arts—music, painting and the dance. A sequence of musical notes *need* not represent anything. It *may* represent the song of the cuckoo, or suggest sadness or passion; but it need not do any of these things. It is the same with painting, though we are often misled by the generally mimetic tradition of European painting. A mark on canvas need not represent anything. It may represent the Cross or a woman's face, but it need not do anything of the sort. It can be merely thick or thin, vertical or horizontal. The media employed by these arts—sounds and visual marks—

[1] *Essay on Man*, p. 187.

are not essentially signs. They are themselves, they need not represent anything else. But the medium of literature is verbal. Literature is made of words. And words are already signs. They stand for something, they represent something already, before literature takes them over. So literature makes use of a medium that is itself already a product of the symbolizing, formative activity. Literature is a symbolic form only in a secondary, derivative sense, for it makes use of a system of symbolic forms that is already in existence—the system that we call language. The world already called into existence by language is used as raw material by literary art. Literature can therefore never be a wholly autonomous symbolic system as music and painting are.

Whatever view we may take of the nature and origin of language, by the time literature gets hold of them words are already signs, representational counters. Literature is therefore essentially mimetic as music and painting are not. There cannot be anything in literature corresponding to nonfigurative painting. And this is why mimetic theories of literature have been so obvious and so prominent.

139. We should be unwise to quarrel with the mimetic orientation of traditional criticism, since it is based on a manifest truth. But we may need to qualify it. An obscure sense that it needs qualifying has been endemic in criticism from the beginning. Poetry is more philosophical than history; it submits the shows of things to the desires of the mind, etc. These and a host of similar pronouncements are all attempts at seeing poetry as in some sense an autonomous symbolic system.

In what sense can this be maintained? To what extent do conventional mimetic assumptions need to be modified or supplemented?

(a) Literature does not work entirely with mimetic or referential methods. The meaning of a poem is its whole

131

complex of structures, not simply its reference. Literature uses words, and words are signs; but in literature they are used as something more than signs. Literature exploits other properties of words besides their referential ones; e.g. their capability of being organized into rhythmical groups, their auditory and muscular suggestions, their fortuitous kinships with other words. Latent and undeveloped in ordinary language, these qualities become decisive in literature. And they fuse with the referential, mimetic properties of words to make of literature a new symbolic system, different from the symbolic system of non-literary language.

(b) Literature uses words, and words are signs, standing for things that we already know in other ways. But literature (indeed language itself) uses these signs with great freedom. It can combine them in ways that are quite foreign to the nature of the things signified. In literature mouths can be blind, light can creak, a man may cross a rainbow bridge, and romantic love can last for ever. Visionary and imaginative experience, 'the irregular combinations of fancy', are part of the substance of literature. The verbal signs, by themselves tied to objects with fixed properties and relations, acquire in literary combination a new freedom of action. In this sense too literature offers a quasi-independent symbolic system.

140. But this independence is never complete. Literature is never in the position of music or the visual arts in making a solitary, unassisted raid on the inarticulate. It works with material that has been articulated already. The numerous attempts, particularly numerous in the last hundred years, to see literature as precisely analogous to the other arts, as an independent symbolic system, collectively comprise the literary theory known as symbolism.

Traditional literary theory sees literature working in the same way as non-literary discourse. The statements of literature are fictions, but within the fictional parenthesis all the ordinary kinds of discourse occur in the ordinary ways. The organizing principles of literature are narrative, description, argument, exhortation and the expression of feeling. And these all involve *saying* something. We can distinguish literature in this respect from ritual or music, which can objectify a complex of experience without *saying* anything.

Symbolist theory tries to assimilate the work of literature to a ritual or a piece of music. 'A poem should not mean but be.'

It is a brave attempt and it needed to be made. But it is an ideal limit, not an actuality. It is only by saying something that a poem can do more than say. It is only through its meaning that a poem can be at all.

141. It was necessary to make the symbolist attempt in the nineteenth century for a variety of related reasons, all of them familiar enough.

The rationalizing tendencies of neo-classicism had reached an impasse. Their possibilities were exhausted and literature could only continue by exploring other methods. The increasing power and prestige of the scientific consciousness threatened to engulf all others, and literature obscurely and instinctively revolted. We see it doing so in German and English romanticism.

But the literature of the early nineteenth century, Romantic literature, was still deeply dedicated to hopes of political and social progress. As the century went on political disenchantment tended to deprive it of this source of vitality; and the unbroken march of science and technology threatened to narrow its sphere of action still farther. Symbolism both intensifies the Romantic revolt and seeks to provide it with an unassailable esoteric philosophy. Hence the exaltation of dream, of various forms of magic and occultism, of non-discursive arts like music and the dance, of non-discursive literary effects such as the symbol (whatever that means) and the image.

Symbolism, seeking to vindicate the claims of literature to be a genuine mode of apprehending reality with its own rights, maximizes those claims. It either tries to cut words loose from their reference altogether—*De la musique avant toute chose*, etc.; or it tries to use the references as talismans and charms (symbols) or as pictures (images).[1]

142. Poetry regarded in this light has a different relation to words from that which is recognized in traditional criticism. It does not use words in the same way; 'même elle ne s'en *sert* pas du tout; je dirai plûtot qu'elle les sert'. A brilliant sketch of the symbolist view of poetry is given by Sartre in the passage, already cited earlier, from which these words are taken. He reconciles this with his highly functional view of literature by distinguishing sharply between *poésie* and *littérature*, between *le poète* and *l'écrivain*. This rather dubious piece of casuistry serves his purpose; and at any rate we know what he means. 'L'écrivain [as distinct from the poet] c'est aux significations qu'il a affaire. Encore faut-il distinguer: l'empire des signes, c'est la prose; la poésie est du côté de la peinture, de la sculpture, de la musique.'[2] But no pre-symbolist critic would have made this distinction. In traditional criticism poetic diction is a matter of selection, refinement or vividness, not of some non-significative quality.

Symbolist criticism then makes a sharp break with former critical theory: it is one of the few major turning-points in our literary thought. What are we to make of it?

[1] See A. G. Lehmann, *The Symbolist Aesthetic in France*, Oxford, 1950; Guy Delfel, *L'Esthétique de Stephane Mallarmé*, Paris, 1951; Maurice Bowra, *The Heritage of Symbolism*, 1951; Joseph Chiari, *Symbolisme from Poe to Mallarmé*, 1956; Edmund Wilson, *Axel's Castle*, 1931, chap. I; Frank Kermode, *Romantic Image*, 1957; G. Hough, *Image and Experience*, 1960.

[2] 'Qu'est ce que la litterature?', *Situations*, II, 63.

143. There is no need either to vindicate or to dispute the creative power that symbolism has released. *Les Illuminations*, *Byzantium*, and *The Waste Land* provide their own testimony. But does post-symbolist criticism account only for symbolist poetry, or has it changed the way we look at poetry in general?

To a large extent it has. It has at least given a new tendency, a new direction to most modern literary interpretation. In the consideration of poetry and prose (Chapter XV) I found myself instinctively adopting, though with some qualifications, the symbolist point of view, feeling as I did so that this was only to say what most modern critics would agree to. How has this worked out in actual critical practice?

The shortest answer is provided by the wide currency of Archibald MacLeish's aphorism, 'A poem should not mean but be.' This implies that the referential content of a poem is only a small part of its totality. No doubt this was always felt and was always implicit in much traditional discussion of poetry. But it was never before so emphatic or so self-aware. And the sense that the total structure of a poem is infinitely more than its referential paraphrasable content has become so vivid in post-symbolist criticism that it has become necessary to provide a far fuller and more intelligible account of the other structural elements and the way they go to form the totality of the work. And because it was necessary it has become possible.

144. To illustrate at all fully the way in which this has been done would be to write a history of modern criticism; and that is not my business. We can only note some general tendencies and a few examples. While literature is regarded as a representation of realities already more or less known, criticism pays much attention to the elucidation of plot, to character-analysis, to historical background and the thought of the age. It tries to show *what* is being represented, and is

relatively weak in illuminating the formative process itself. Goethe, Coleridge, Bradley all discuss the character and actions of Hamlet as something that could in principle be known without the play. For the post-symbolist Wilson Knight a Shakespearean play is an 'expanded metaphor', a symbolic whole in which the imagery, the rhythms, the minute verbal structure are as important as character-in-action—which cannot in any case be conceived apart from the poetic form in which alone it subsists. Livingstone Lowes, a critic of this century who was nevertheless quite untouched by the active literary thought of his time, can give a wonderfully complete account of the source-material of *The Ancient Mariner*, but is at a loss to give any notion of the essence of the poem, and talks helplessly about enchantment and aimless magnificence. While Robert Penn Warren, a post-symbolist critic if ever there was one, can give a not indisputable but brilliantly illuminating interpretation of *The Ancient Mariner* as a total symbolic pattern, considering not the material out of which it is made, but the use which is made of it. William Empson, by exploiting the concept of ambiguity and multiple meaning, can elucidate the structure of passages that had formerly seemed either to defy analysis or not to require it.

We can distinguish three stages here.

(a) That of traditional criticism, in which the meaning of a poem is its referential meaning, what it 'says', *plus* some more or less unanalysed quality added by poetic diction, refinement or vividness of language, the grand style, or what not.

(b) The symbolist phase in which the poem is a unique revelation, communicating nothing but its own essence. Its efficacy may be ascribed to 'music', to what it does *not* say, or to some supernatural power; but in any case we are not encouraged to analyse its procedure.

(c) The phase reached in modern criticism, where the symbolist view of the poem persists but the ban on analysis is removed. The critic tries to display the structure of the revelation, the means by which the unique essence is realized.

•   •   •

145. The connection between this post-symbolist criticism
and symbolist aesthetics is far from obvious, for their tone is
so unlike. The utterances of modern critics, with their passion
for explication, seem totally opposed to those of Poe,
Baudelaire, Mallarmé and Yeats, with their passion for
mystery, the evasive and the inexplicable. But most modern
criticism in fact represents an analytical exploration of the
symbolist point of view—the view of the poem as a symbolic
structure, not reproducing a pre-existing reality, but calling
into being, by a complex of means, many of them non-
discursive and non-referential, a new reality.

The really startling thing in modern criticism is to be
told what the literary work is 'about'. When Humphry House
did this, as he often did, it came as something of a shock.
And a critic like Yvor Winters, who adheres firmly to the
discursive, referential and logical point of view, is markedly
out of step with most of his contemporaries.

146. It may be that the symbolists themselves were right.
They are certainly better reading than their successors. *L'Art
Romantique*, Mallarmé's *Divagations*, Yeats's essays are
works of genius; the writings of modern commentators are
works of talent. It may be true that poetry presents a system
of hidden correspondences that really pervade the universe. It
may be true that poetic symbols derive their power from the
action of spiritual powers. In that case much recent literary
interpretation would be tautologous—repeating in its own
terms what has been revealed once and for all; or arid—
subjecting to analysis what is only fertile as an unanalysed
whole; or pointless—trying to say what cannot be said.
Wovon man nicht sprechen kann darüber muss man schweigen.

Then the only task of criticism would be to distinguish the
authentic from the inauthentic and to leave the authentic to
speak for itself. But that is literature for a better world than
ours. We need the help of the discursive intellect. To be more

hopeful and more generous to a real intellectual endeavour, the new critical orientation that we have described has at least corrected a balance. It has opened up new areas to the literary intelligence, and it has brought with it great advances in critical technique. It is probable therefore that it has effected a permanent change in the literary consciousness.

It needs qualification, however, in two ways.

(a) It is a supplement to other methods of interpretation, not a substitute for them. Poetry is 'about' something, about something that is not poetry, because it uses words, and words are representational signs. Poetry remains therefore always linked to representation—partly free from it but never wholly free. A play of Shakespeare can indeed be seen as an expanded metaphor, a total symbolic structure. But it is also a representation of character in action. And it will always be most natural to most men to think of it as a representation of character in action. If the common reader or the unsophisticated playgoer tends to think of Hamlet as existing in some sense outside the play he is strictly wrong and his habits will be offensive to purists. But he is not very damagingly wrong; and he is in his own way saying more about the play than any pure analyst of themes and images can do.

(b) The conception of the poem as a symbolic structure calling into being a new reality represents an ideal state, a notional purity to which literature aspires but never wholly attains. Music may attain it, and certain kinds of visual art, for their symbolism is in principle wholly free. Literature can never wholly do so, for its symbolism is tied to a reality already represented in language, an untransmutable residue which can be used, but can never be sublimed away. Sartre's idea of poetry as capable of an ideal purity while 'literature' is irremediably 'engaged' is a false dichotomy, The dialectic of freedom and engagement is present in all literature, prose or poetry, now one factor dominant, now the other. Ultimately it is the same as the dialectic of formal and moral considerations that we discussed in an earlier part of this essay.

Literature keeps us in *les jardins de cet astre* while showing us *l'azur* that lies around them. It is foolish to make a hierarchy of the arts; each has its own kingdom. But literature by aspiring to an ideal purity and freedom which it can never quite attain affords a completer symbol of the human situation than any of the other arts alone can do.

CHAPTER TWENTY

MYTH AND ARCHETYPE I

147. Recent criticism has shown great interest in the relation of poetry to myth. This is a revived interest. It is as old as Plato's *Phaedrus*, it continues in the Neoplatonists, it reappears in the mythographers of the Renaissance, and it acquires a new force with Herder and the German Romantics.

Yet the main stream of purely literary criticism, derived from Aristotle, is largely neglectful of it. Aristotle seems to have forgotten the mythic origins of Greek tragedy, and explains the recurrence of the great mythological stories by the fact that it is only in a few families that such terrible deeds and sufferings have occurred (*Poetics* 13). From this comes the habit of taking the mythical element in literature for granted. Myth is regarded as a component of literature, providing some striking plots and a great deal of ornamental imagery. (In my schooldays you were supposed to learn about myth in order to explain 'allusions'.)

The modern critical interest in myth derives partly from the anthropologists and psychologists (Frazer, Freud and Jung), and partly from the philosophy of Cassirer, continued in the English-speaking world by Suzanne Langer. From these diverse influences (which it is not our business here to trace historically) a new orientation has been given to basically traditional criticism, and a new school of what is actually called 'myth-criticism' has arisen.

Excluding as far as possible its epistemological, anthropological and psychological *Urgrund* we must try to survey the literary importance of this way of thought.

148. Modern mythological critics are far from regarding myth as a mere contributory stream; they regard it as the matrix from which all literature springs. This requires some consideration.

For Cassirer, myth is pre-linguistic, or at least an independent symbolical system developing parallel with the development of language.[1] However this may be, it is not of much use to the literary critic. The critic cannot concern himself with myth until it has been expressed in language. It is true that myth is not bound to language, for it may be painted, acted or danced.[2] It may be expressed in ritual. But it does not concern literature until it has attained a linguistic form. Ritual acts may precede language, as a quasi-automatic response to emotionally-charged situations. They may even be found in the animal world. But 'even the most intelligent partridge cannot tell even the most absurd story explaining why it drums in the mating season'.[3] And for literature myth implies a story.

149. Even when it has attained linguistic form and crystallized into a story, myth is not yet literature—for it is not bound to any particular verbal structure. The same myth may have many widely differing verbal expressions. This has been so from the earliest times and the tendency has persisted. Myth rarely achieves a definite literary formulation. Apart from its great literary embodiments myth has always been recorded and pursued in miscellanies and compendia of little or no literary pretensions. Even the learned poets of the Renaissance used Boccaccio's *De Genealogia Deorum* and the work of Natalis Comes. Schoolboys of my generation had known the myths in Kingsley's *Heroes* and Bullfinch's *Age of*

[1] *Language and Myth*, trans. Suzanne Langer, New York, 1946, chap. I.
[2] Suzanne Langer, *Feeling and Form*, 1953, p. 274.
[3] Northrop Frye, *Anatomy of Criticism*, 1957, p. 107.

Fable long before they met them in Virgil and Milton, and followed them up in classical dictionaries long after.

150. This shows myth as living on side by side with literature and entering into relations with it; but it does not show it as the original root from which all literature sprang.

The nineteenth century however began to develop this idea. George Eliot's Mr. Casaubon was trying to write a Key to all the Mythologies, and Frazer actually wrote it. *The Golden Bough* may not be the *passe-partout* that it once appeared; but it offers an explanation of all mythology as concealed seasonal and fertility ritual. This was eagerly seized on by both poets and critics as providing a positive ground and justification for the use of fading myths to which they were still deeply attached. What had begun to look like unfunctional ornament was seen to have a real foundation, and acquired a new lease of life.

This movement was seconded by the psychologists. Freud found the origin of the Oedipus myth in the universal familial situation, found parallels to it in the dreams of his modern patients, and discovered it lurking at the heart of many works of literature. The living germ of works of the imagination was found in unconscious mental processes. What is more, Freud himself said it was not he who had revealed the unconscious but the artists and poets. Jung, the dissident disciple who abandoned Freud's pan-sexualism, broadened the basis of this way of thought and traced a large range of literary motifs to universal, archaic and forgotten psychic archetypes. (The term archetype is his; we use the word *myth* for the story, *archetype* for the single motif.)

The way was now open for a new approach to literature. Instead of seeing it as a mimesis of empirical experience it could now be seen as a symbolization of ancient and deep-rooted tendencies of the human mind—tendencies which have had their primary expression in myth. On this view the literary mimesis of empirical experience is only a screen for older and far more deeply-rooted psychic material.[1]

151. A sharp break was thus made with previous critical tradition. Hitherto most formal criticism had developed relatively independent notions of literary form, seen as something directed to an aesthetic end, not closely related to other areas of experience. Most moral criticism had a strong mimetic tendency, relating the characters and events in literature to those that were familiar in actual life. Myth-criticism on the other hand sees literary form not as chosen for an aesthetic end but as dictated by psychological compulsions. And it sees characters and events in literature not as imitations of similar characters and events in experience, but as symbolizations of archaic, otherwise inarticulate responses to certain archetypal situations.

The new habits of thought rapidly become established. Characters in fictional works cease to be 'just representations of nature' and become embodiments of a few mythical constants. Any young man who dies becomes a dying god, related to Attis, Adonis and Osiris. Any girl who is carried off and comes back again becomes Persephone; and any heroine who is badly treated by one character and rescued by another becomes Andromeda. Anyone who goes looking for anything becomes a participant in the 'quest-myth'. Any tragedy is the rite of winter and any comedy is the rite of spring. If as soon happens the Christian myth is taken into the corpus the young man who is a dying god also becomes a figure of Christ crucified; the victorious rescuer becomes

---

[1] We cannot here even give references to the immense literature on this subject; the only satisfactory beginning is to read Frazer, Freud and Jung *in extenso*. As a fragmentary exemplification of the secondary discussions we might cite: Jessie L. Weston, *From Ritual to Romance*, Cambridge, 1920; Maud Bodkin, *Archetypal Patterns in Poetry*, Oxford, 1934; Lord Raglan, *The Hero: a Study in Tradition, Myth and Drama*, 1937; Joseph Campbell, *The Hero with a Thousand Faces*, New York, 1 956; Northrop Frye, *Anatomy of Criticism*, 1957.

Christ the vanquisher of Satan; all gardens become Eden, and all happy endings are symbols of redemption.

There are two questions to be answered about this kind of mythological identification: how far is it to be accepted; and what has criticism to gain by it?

152. To a large extent it must be accepted. The method has been institutionalized to the point of parody (any graduate student can be taught to recognize a dying god); but the candid critic cannot refuse to recognize the results of nearly a hundred years of anthropological and psychological observation. And since this observation has been one of the major intellectual movements of our time it must become absorbed into his consciousness. This great body of work has united to make us see, more clearly than has ever been possible before, certain uniformities of symbolism, some the property of a single culture, some apparently common to man as man. We see as we have never done before that certain patterns of mythic narrative, certain archetypal characters and situations, tend to recur, under a multiplicity of disguises, in age after age and country after country. We are still far from possessing Mr. Casaubon's Key to all the Mythologies, but the equipment that we have enables us to perceive a whole network of patterns and connections that were formerly invisible.

This does not entail discipleship in any particular school or commit the critic to any particular theory of human behaviour. No one is obliged to accept Freudian or Jungian psychology; no one (we are told) ought to accept the argument of *The Golden Bough* as it stands; but it would be wilful blindness in a literary critic to reject the immense tract of new knowledge, the new possibilities of correlation, that such researches have brought to light.

However, this is far from assuring us that myth is the universal mother from which all literature springs. Myth is a primitive and an enduring element in literature; but we are not justified on that account in making it the basic constitutive factor of literature as such. This is to commit the genetic fallacy—to explain a developed form in terms of its origins. Even if we grant what we need not, that myth is the cause of literature, this would be a piece of misplaced scientism. For literary explanations are in terms of understanding, not of cause and effect. We have learnt, I believe with certainty, that myth is a constant and functional element in literature, not a mere decoration or survival. But what weight we are to give it in relation to other elements remains an entirely open question. And while this is so the individual critic is free to answer it according to his own interests.

153. The question of what criticism has to gain from these insights is more difficult. Any new knowledge must make a difference; and most of what we are discussing is new knowledge. There was simply not enough anthropological information available to make fruitful speculation on these matters possible until recently. But what does it tell us?

Fundamentally something reductive. It offers us a scheme of classification. Literary works which do not appear to be related can be seen as belonging to a single type. A number of such groupings might in the end cover the whole literary field. They would then present an alternative to the old literary kinds, and we should have a new literary taxonomy, more comprehensive, it might be claimed, and more soundly based than the old. Leaving aside the question of whether so complete a scheme is actually available we must recognize this as a promising line of enquiry.

It would have its inconveniences. Such a scheme would cut across our accustomed literary categories. The myth of Persephone, for example (the myth of the death and rebirth of spring), may appear in any literary form—lyric, dramatic or narrative, prose or verse. We may question whether a class that contains *All's Well, The Rape of the Lock, Pamela,* and half the soap-operas on the air is of great utility to criticism.[1] The work of cobblers, meat-pie makers, veterinary surgeons and Hindu priests all depend on the archetypal figure of the cow; but they cannot otherwise be brought into any very fruitful relation.

Do we know significantly more about an individual work of literature by putting it in its appropriate mythic class? Not much. We see it in a new light by recognizing its unsuspected relatives. But this one rather blunt and unselective tool gives us no additional means of analysing its structure or judging its value. Myth-criticism is not concerned with value; the classic example of the anima archetype, according to Jung, is found in Rider Haggard's *She*. In its application to any particular literary case myth-criticism turns out to be curiously disappointing. It tells us much of interest, but not what we really want to know. When we are told that a number of obviously different stories are variants of the same type we may on investigation suspend our disbelief; but we may also feel that we are not much better informed than we were before. I do not think it possible that myth-criticism is a bogus science, like phrenology or hand-reading; but it is possible, for all its allurements, that it has less to contribute than is often supposed.

154. Yet the allurements are undeniable. Can we say that a way of talking about literature which is manifestly interesting and attractive, which reveals new relations and perspectives, which brings its subject-matter into relation with other important fields of enquiry, is still of minor critical importance? There seems an awkward paradox here; and it may be that we are merely resisting disturbance to old habits, or that new procedures have been imperfectly absorbed.

It is clear at any rate that there are fields where myth-criticism has nothing to say. It can tell us nothing about

[1] See *Anatomy of Criticism*, p. 183.

verbal art—and literature is an art of words. It cannot assist
us in the judgment of value—and works of literature are
made to be objects of value. The explanation of the paradox
is this—that myth-criticism in the pure state is not essentially
concerned with literature. It uses literature as the object for
what is essentially an anthropological study. Its fundamental
interest is in the transmigration of symbolic forms. It finds
its material in literature, but it might find it anywhere else;
and it is at heart indifferent whether the literature it uses is
of merit or not.

This is not to discredit or depreciate such a study, which
obviously has its own rights. It is not to deny its usefulness
as an auxiliary to criticism of other kinds. The imaginative
student of literature is not likely to depreciate the literary
study of myth, for he finds it an abiding source of interest.
But so far as he is a student of literature he finds it on the
border, not in the centre of his own activity.

CHAPTER TWENTY-ONE

MYTH AND ARCHETYPE II

155. To be fair to the mythological mode of criticism we should inspect it in a concrete developed form. Neglecting the epigoni and the lunatic fringe we shall take the system of Northrop Frye. System is the word; for what he has attempted is nothing less than an analysis of literature as a total coherent symbolic structure.[1]

Frye cuts off his myth-criticism as far as possible from its anthropological and psychological roots and considers literature as a self-contained system. He defines myth simply as a story in which 'some characters are superhuman beings who do things that "only happen in stories"; hence a conventionalised or stylised narrative—not fully adapted to plausibility or "realism"' (p. 366). But he designedly does not consider its origins from the anthropological point of view. And he defines archetype as 'a symbol, usually an image, which recurs often enough in literature to be recognisable as an element of one's literary experience as a whole' (p. 365). But he does not consider the psychological necessities that make it recurrent. He carefully avoids saying that the myths and archetypes found in literature are historically descended from originals in ritual, primitive myth or the unconscious. 'To the literary critic, ritual is the *content* of dramatic action, not the source of origin of it. . . . It does not matter two pins to the literary critic whether such a ritual had any existence or not. . . . The critic, therefore, is concerned only with the ritual or dream patterns which are actually in what he is studying, however they got there' (p. 109).

Methodologically this is a great convenience; but it can-

[1] See *Anatomy of Criticism, passim*. The principal places are pp. 33–71, 131–293. Page references in what follows are all to the *Anatomy*.

not be supposed that Frye would ever have thought in terms of myth and archetype at all without the previous existence of anthropological and psychological researches. And he says in another place that 'the structural principles of literature are as closely related to mythology and comparative religion as those of painting to geometry' (p. 134). This seems to claim that myth provides literature with its formal structure, and it seems inconsistent with the previous statement that ritual (which may be regarded as pre-literary myth) provides drama with its *content*. But however that may be, the way is opened for his view that all literature is displaced myth, i.e. that it is not a mimesis of experience, and not therefore essentially bound to plausibility and realism. Clearly what is at work here is the notion of mythology as a coherent pre-literary system, and of literature as another coherent system structurally derived from it.

156. The relation between myth and literature is effected by what Frye, borrowing a Freudian term, calls 'displacement'.[1] The original mythological stories, autonomous, non-realistic, springing from the basic tendencies of the human mind, enter into various degrees of relation with realism, and are accommodated to the representation of ordinary experience. The god becomes a hero or a sage, the scapegoat becomes a suffering human being, the magical autonomy of the figures of myth becomes subdued to natural and social necessity. The displacement is least in romance, which still retains many of the characteristics of myth. It becomes greater as we pass through heroic literature to what is ordinarily called 'realism'. Here the mythic patterns persist, but disguised and concealed, like wishes in dreams. What we are ordinarily aware of is the mimesis of actual experience. But it is still, according to Frye, the mythic patterns that dictate the structure even of 'realistic' literary works. Tragedy and comedy

[1] See also 'Myth, Fiction and Displacement', in *Fables of Identity*, New York, 1963, pp. 21–38.

for instance retain their basic formulas whether they are in the mode of fairy-tale or the mode of naturalism.

157. This bald summary must serve to represent a brilliant and persuasive argument that must be read in full to be properly appreciated. When it has been properly appreciated its broad outline is bound, I believe, to become a part of our normal critical apparatus. It is not, however, a panacea for all critical ills or a substitute for all other equipment; and its elaborations shade into fantasy. We should try now to indicate its virtues and its limits.

Frye's system attracts aesthetically by its logic and its comprehensiveness. Practically its great virtue is that it puts 'realism' in its proper place—as a particular development of literature occurring in particular historical circumstances. The normal mimetic bias of most traditional criticism tends to present literature as aspiring steadily towards the representation of actuality—'lifelikeness' in character drawing, 'probability' in incident. Historically this is quite untenable. If we look at literature over its whole extent, representational plausibility of this kind is only one method out of many. It appears intermittently, and it may disappear again at any time, as it seems to be doing both in drama and fiction at present. There are large tracts of literature (historically speaking the largest) in which it plays a subordinate part. Frye's account of the matter shows literature as what it really is, as what Baumgarten called it—a 'heterocosm', another world, related to the real world by analogy, but not, in general, an imitation of the real world. As we live in a literary climate that has until recently been dominated by realism, and as the old habits still persist, it is particularly important that this should be brought before us.

158. But there are qualifications to be made. Perhaps they are largely a matter of balance and emphasis. Even though we admit the validity of Frye's general picture it must also be admitted that as soon as literature becomes literature at all— as soon, that is, as the mythic stories acquire specific literary forms—the mimesis of actual experience also begins. From the start it takes its place by the side of myth as a constitutive principle. In Greek tragedy, which is still very near to myth, we meet with individualized characters, not wholly stylized functional figures. Supernatural interventions are confined on the whole to prologues and epiphanies, the main action proceeding in an ordinary causal sequence. In Shakespearean comedy it is true that the dénouement is commonly brought about by fairy-tale devices that are completely implausible in the light of ordinary experience: yet the plays live largely through our sympathy with the characters as acting and suffering human beings, each with its individual essence. Rosalind is different from Viola, and both are different from Perdita, whatever mythic archetype they commonly represent. And so on. The mimetic point of view (what we might call the Bradleyan point of view) has been resolutely taken by the vast majority of common readers. In comparison with it myth-criticism is one of the dogmatisms of learning. Frye has written beautifully and illuminatingly on comedy, Shakespearean comedy in particular; but it can be fairly said that he has brought out the characteristics of the type only by a pretty cavalier treatment of the actual goings-on in any particular play.

159. A juster view of the relation of myth to literature would be that myth represents one pole of literary creation; the other pole being experience, reality, 'nature', our sense of how things happen. Ever since literature became literature the two have existed in a state of dialectical tension—on the one side the archaic outlines of a relatively few persistent and

unchanging stories, on the other the inexhaustible flux of experience. This is not as Frye would have it, a relation of form and content. Both are parts of content.[1] It is not that a mythic container is filled up with representational material. Mythic elements mingle and fuse with mimetic ones, and both are contained (though this is not the right metaphor) in a form that is dictated by purely literary considerations—the form of the romantic epic, of the Racinian tragedy, of the picaresque novel. Frye's brilliant analysis of comedy is not a purely structural analysis: it also discusses the characters, the emotions, the experiential content. Myth is not the geometry of literature; it is part of its material. And it can no more provide the basis for a structural philosophy of literature than any other part of literary material.

To found the structure of literature on myth, as Frye and others would do, is no more adequate than to found it on 'realism', as the unanalytical critic of today or yesterday is apt to do. Both lead to contradictions; and as the contradictions of an omnicompetent realism have by now been sufficiently remarked on, we will proceed to illustrate some of the contradictions of the notion of omnicompetent myth. They will lead us to suppose that myth is indeed an abiding element in literature but that it has not the decisive, formative importance that myth-criticism would ascribe to it.

160. If myth is to provide the structure of literature it must itself have a consistent and intelligible structure. Otherwise we are explaining *obscurum per obscurius* and achieving nothing. Frye takes a roughly *Golden Bough* view of the nature of myth—that its contemplative foundation is the cycle of the seasons, its pragmatic foundations fertility and nutrition. But this has long been discredited as the universal key to all the mythologies. It has no more exclusive rights than

---

[1] We may think that Frye partly suspected this in the unguarded remark quoted earlier, that 'ritual is the *content* of dramatic action'.

the Neoplatonic mythography of the Renaissance, the solar myth that was fashionable in the nineteenth century, the pansexualism of Freud or the quasi-religious system of Jung. Frye's procedure displays the typical literary man's tendency to borrow concepts from another discipline and to get them only partly right. The result of trying to find a serious anthropological foundation for literature would be a far more complex affair—and far too confusing to provide a structural analysis that could be of use to criticism.

As it is, Frye's structural analysis is confusing enough. The seasonal myth is mysteriously fused with the mythology of the Bible, itself seen through Blakean and Swedenborgian spectacles. We have heaven and hell, each with its appropriate imagery, and an intricately (though incompletely) analysed imagery of human experience in between. Superimposed on these are four basic 'myths' (the word now being used in a different sense)—comedy, romance, tragedy and satire, described charmingly but fancifully as the myths of spring, summer, autumn and winter. Each of these is subdivided into six types; and even if these were clearly distinguished from one another, which they are not, we begin at this point to feel that the complications of the system outweigh its utility.

Specific details are handled in an extremely arbitrary fashion. Hilda of *The Marble Faun* is, or is something near to, 'a dove-goddess like Venus' (p. 137). Well, she is closely associated with doves, but in what other respect is this pallid New England anchoress like *alma Venus*? Or *Venus toute entière à sa proie attaché* for that matter. The organizing ideas of romance, we are told, are chastity and magic (p. 153). Magic, indeed; but chastity? One does not like to place oneself in what Mr. Frye calls the oh-come-now school of criticism, but oh come now, all the same. Guinevere? Yseult? Angelica? A remarkably high proportion of European romances are in fact about adultery. Other examples of this high-handed dealing with the facts are not lacking.

Everywhere there are brilliant *apercus*; and the whole essay on comedy, more fully developed than the treatment of any of the other 'myths', is an independent contribution to criticism of the utmost value. But it is not easy to think of it as an authentic part of the comprehensive structural scheme. And in other parts the scheme looks like a free fantasia, only loosely related to what is supposed to be its material.

161. In effect, Frye has written his own compendious *Golden Bough*, using literary rather than anthropological material. It is a highly personal *Golden Bough*, suffused with the quality of his own imagination. The whole 'Theory of Myths' chapter in the *Anatomy* is a beautiful and intricate imaginative construction. It is itself poetry, one of the cases, not very common, where what sets out to be criticism turns into imaginative literature in its own right. It is one of the real visionary achievements of our time, a vision of the European imagination at work; and to that extent the cavils of the oh-come-now school, which I have ungraciously exemplified, are powerless against it. But it is not criticism in the sense of being a usable tool. And when we see (as we now often do) the results of putting this beautiful and ingenious piece of apparatus into the hands of those who have less imagination, vitality and literary experience than Frye himself we see it losing its self-subsistent charm without acquiring much instrumental utility.

There are good reasons for believing that if Mr. Frye cannot make the system work no one else can. Myth-criticism offers us a new and valuable approach to some literary questions—an approach that has been too long neglected. But its use is limited. It frees us from the bonds of a too-dominant realism. It puts the individual literary work into the long perspective of the developing human imagination. This brings about an expansion of the imaginative horizon. But in the end the task of interpretation and judgment, the understanding of the work on its own terms, all remains to be done, by other means.

162. What we do learn after reading the mythological criticism of today is the enduring vitality of mythical structures *independent of belief*. We have been apt to think of certain recurring, more or less magical narrative patterns as part of religion and therefore objects of belief; and of certain others as parts of mythology and therefore mere decoration. It would seem that as far as literature is concerned this distinction cannot be drawn.

The word myth is itself ambiguous. On the one hand it implies stories that were believed—thought to provide explanations of the origin of the world, natural phenomena, etc. Equally it tends to imply stories that are not now believed. To speak of 'the Christian myth' tends to imply it is a fable like any other. But belief or disbelief has nothing to do with the matter. The Christian myths which are believed and the pagan ones which are not lie side by side in *Lycidas*, without any distinction. Camus reverend sire is no more or less real than St. Peter, and we are offered no preference between the two versions of Lycidas's final destiny—one as a pagan genius of the shore and the other as a saint in the Christian heaven.

Lycidas may be regarded as a late product of Renaissance syncretism and so not typical. But similar situations are general. The Padre Eterno in Tasso *suddenly notices* that all the devils have got out of hell and are helping the Saracens:[1] the omnipotent and omniscient ruler of the universe, the object of an all-embracing faith, is for the moment conceived as one of the half-fanciful anthropomorphic deities of the Gentiles. Even in very early mythologies alternative creation myths, alternative genealogies of the gods make their appearance. If one was true the others were false; yet there seems to have been no conflict between them. The solution is that none was believed in any exclusive sense. All might be accepted as symbolic realizations of complex states of thought, feeling and sensation. Belief as we commonly use the term seems to be a product of Semitic religious exclusiveness reinforced by Christian institutions. No one died to assert the

[1] *Gerusalemme Liberata*, IX, 58.

divine parentage of Orpheus. And it is the non-Christian attitude in which myths are impartially entertained, rather than the Christian one in which they are believed or disbelieved, that is the normal habit of literature.

Those who maintain that the Christian myth is different from all others are right—not because it is 'truer' than any other, but because it was believed in a different way. And some critics have thought it unsuitable for literary purposes on that account (Cinthio, Boileau). Yet the natural tendency of literature is to slip back into the older mode of symbolic acceptance.

CHAPTER TWENTY-TWO

ORGANIC FORM: A METAPHOR

163. Since the Romantic age much use has been made in criticism of the idea of 'organic form'. Analogies are drawn between a literary work and a natural organism. We need not doubt that this is a convenient way of talking; but does it cover any precise idea? We should enquire into the nature of this conception.

In neo-classic criticism most of the analogies for the process of poetic creation were constructive or mechanical: a psychology that built up the mental life from simple units of sensation was inclined to see the building up of a poem in the same way—as a *putting together* of images derived from sensation. The classic account of this process is to be found in Coleridge's definition of Fancy (*Biog. Lit.*, XIII), which comprises pretty well the whole creative process as the previous age had understood it.

German Romantic critics rejected this way of thinking and evolved the notion of 'organic form', by which the work is seen growing to its own inherent form, like a plant from the seed. This they contrasted with 'mechanic form', greatly to the disadvantage of the latter. Various illustrations of the dichotomy were given; this, for example, by A. W. Schlegel:

'Form is mechanical when, through external influence, it is communicated to any material merely as an accidental addition, without reference to its quality; as, for example, when we give a particular shape to a soft mass that it may retain the same after its induration. Organical form, [on the contrary], is innate; it unfolds itself from within, and acquires its determination along with the complete development of the germ.'[1]

[1] A. W. Schlegel, *Lectures on Dramatic Literature*, trans. John Black, 1815, II, 94. Copied in almost the same words by Coleridge, in *Literary Remains*, II, pp. 68–69.

Organic form thus makes its first appearance as a special kind of form, not as a special way of talking about literary form in general. Shakespeare's, for instance, is 'organic form'. The idea is originally called upon as a justification of Shakespeare, and as a defence of his supposed 'formlessness' against neo-classical standards. Blake exalts the Gothic over the Greek in the same way: 'Grecian is Mathematic Form; Gothic is Living Form.' It is easy to see the polemical utility of this in the Romantic age, but what is its real critical value?

164. Organic form is introduced to us as a special kind of form—a specially honourable kind. The appeal of the metaphor is easy to see; it makes us think of poems growing like flowers instead of being made like mud pies or Meccano models. But what is the real distinction? How are we to determine whether the form of a work of literature has been externally imposed or is co-natural with its conception? There does not seem to be any way of doing this. The idea of 'mechanic form' can become a pejorative metaphorical stick with which to beat any form one happens to dislike; that of 'organic form' an honorific metaphor for any form one happens to approve. But there is no evidence that could be brought to show that the form of *Phèdre* is less organic, or arises less from the nature of the material, than that of *Othello*. It proceeds by a different set of conventions, and that is all. The interests of criticism can be advanced by describing and differentiating these conventions, but the organic-mechanic distinction gives us little help in doing this. It is a label, and a label that begs many questions; but it does little to describe, delimit, or define anything.

Later the idea of organic form is extended to cover all genuine poetry.

165. The idea of a poem as an organism suggests first that it is a natural growth, and so emphasizes spontaneity against conscious craftsmanship. It also suggests the subordination of parts to the whole, the typical 'organic' character that the parts have meaning only in relation to the whole.

The first is part of the psychology of artistic creation, and so strictly external to criticism—certainly not open to inspection by critical methods. The second includes no content that is not implicitly present in our earlier conceptions of integrity and consonance. All that has happened is that we have introduced a new metaphor.

The historical consequences of the new metaphor were very extensive;[1] and it may still be found a more sympathetic analogy for the integrity of a work of art than any other. It calls attention to one side of the dialectic of artistic creation—that it is a partly unconscious 'natural' process, at the expense of the other—that it is also under the control of the will and judgment. But it is only a metaphor, and it brings about only a change of emphasis. Whether we speak of a poem as a construction or a natural growth, it is still to be seen as a unity, composed of parts that only have meaning in relation to the whole. This is as apparent in Aristotle as it is in Coleridge. Aristotle's account of the plot with its beginning, middle and end, its change of fortune, its peripeteias and discoveries arising from the action and serving to advance it, is only a particular example of the organic multeity-in-unity that is Coleridge's fundamental structural principle.

The principle is the same, but a new terminology has served better to appeal to the interests of a changed historical phase. And it is the business of critical theory to discover where possible the general principle that will cover more than one historical phase. For this reason many of the great revolutions that loom largely in the *history* of literary ideas make only a slight appearance among its *principles*.

[1] Discussed at length from this point of view in M. H. Abrams, *The Mirror and the Lamp*, 1957. See especially pp. 167–77, 218–25.

.   .   .

166. The situation just described illustrates a disconcerting feature of critical language—the power of metaphor. For various cultural and social reasons a new metaphor comes to seem appropriate as the embodiment of a well-known and well-established critical concept. This inaugurates a whole new critical vocabulary, a new tone and a new set of images. This new outfit of critical terms looks extremely unlike the old, and as a rule is intended to; but in many cases its actual content will be found to be far less novel than is supposed.

Much critical argument arises out of these changes in metaphor and imagery—in particular historical circumstances justifiably, even necessarily so. But it is often argument about what tone of voice we ought to talk in rather than about what we ought to say.

The history of criticism must take note of these changes of terminology and tone; the study of critical principles should as far as possible override them, or rather subsume them in ideas of greater generality.

As for the practice of criticism—no doubt it will use the metaphors that are current. But to be effective it must avoid being bemused by them. And the way to do this is by specific description and the comparison of one work with another. Critical metaphors are rhetorical devices, and often suggestive starting-points, but they cannot settle anything.

167. When we are discussing critical theory, then, it is important to distinguish terminology that introduces a new principle from terminology that merely introduces a change of taste. To talk of myth as the structural foundation of literature does, I believe, for good or ill, really introduce a new principle into criticism. To talk as Wordsworth did of poetic diction, for all his challenging air, introduces no new principle. Wordsworth's social orientation, his chosen area of experience, his rhetorical preferences, are all distinct from, say, Johnson's. But in principle Wordsworth and Johnson are

not too far apart. Wordsworth's 'selection of the language really used by men', the idea that the language of poetry is a purified version of common speech, points in pretty much the same direction as Johnson's 'words too familiar or too remote defeat the purpose of the poet'. And we find them uniting to attack the poetic language of Gray, for the same reasons.

A change of taste of the greatest historical importance, one that must be taken note of both by the historian of poetry and the historian of criticism, turns out not to be based on any significant change of principle. So it is with the notion of organic form.

168. I should expect this to be doubted. It may be said, for example, that the 'organic' metaphor introduces an aesthetic relativism, which is an authentically new principle. Since each work is to develop according to its own inner nature there is no possibility of reducing all to a single norm. But this conclusion is not entailed by the metaphor (if indeed any conclusion can be entailed by a metaphor). If this conclusion is drawn (as it often was) it is only because men had other reasons for wanting to draw it. It could as plausibly be said (and was by Coleridge) that all natural organisms develop according to a single law; or that it is the business of every rose to become the idea of the rose, every dandelion to become the perfect dandelion. And this, starting from the same metaphor, would bring us back to the old anti-romantic, neo-classic theory of kinds.

169. We have here a brief illustration of the difficulty of critical language. To a greater extent than philosophy or discussion of the visual arts literary discussion has lacked a precise and specialized vocabulary. Critics have often been

poets or men of letters who have satisfied a limited creative impulse in their criticism. Metaphors that are vivid, evocative but multiple in their applications are preferred to disinfected technical terms. The language of criticism has tended always towards idiosyncrasy, variety and proliferation. We need not regret this; it would be much duller to read if it were not so. But the variety probably covers a greater simplicity of principle than is generally realized.

CHAPTER TWENTY-THREE

THE NATURE OF CRITICAL ARGUMENT

170. It should now be possible to say something about the nature of literary discussion. Obviously it is multifarious. The discussion of literary questions employs arguments and evidence of many different kinds, and much of the confusion in criticism is caused by failure to recognize this. Too many critical arguments take a form in which A says a certain object is blue and B says no, it is not blue, it is anthropomorphic. Naturally no very profitable conclusion is reached. It is hoped that some of these situations have been clarified in our preceding discussions.

171. Some of the statements in critical discourse can be simply true or false. When the appropriate means of verification are available the true state of the case can be established; and criticism can to that extent be progressive. From the end of the eighteenth century onwards the dating of Shakespeare's plays began to be worked out with a fair degree of accuracy. A critical view of Shakespeare's poetic development then became possible that was simply not possible before.

This amounts to saying that some literary arguments are about matters of fact, and some literary scholarship is concerned with establishing the facts—e.g. the dates of an author's works, the priority between different versions of a work, the authorship of works whose provenance is doubtful.

But matters of fact do not, for good or ill, play as large a part in criticism as in many other branches of knowledge. Factual considerations cannot provide answers to most of the questions (questions of interpretation and judgment) that we most wanted answered. And most of the important facts are not in doubt, and are quite properly taken for granted. Many facts about the Book of Job, for example, are in doubt—its date, its authorship, its integrity as a composition. But the major literary fact, whoever wrote it and however many alterations and interpolations it has been subject to, is its existence for over two thousand years in the form in which we have it. It has profoundly influenced the literary consciousness in that form; and that therefore is what exists for literature. This is not to depreciate the historical scholarship that would clear up such uncertainties; it may be of great importance to theology and religious history; but it cannot be of the first importance to literature. Similarly with the authorship of Shakespeare's plays. If it could be proved that a multiplicity of hands had been at work in what is attributed to Shakespeare the major literary fact would still be the existence of the plays as we know them. 'The *Iliad* wasn't written by Homer but by another gentleman of the same name.' The old joke has its point.

Some of the facts discovered by bibliographical science are critically irrelevant; and much textual criticism today has developed a technical skill far beyond the stage where it offers any substantial literary gains.

172. There is some room for controversy about the methods by which literary facts are established. So far as they depend on what is called 'external evidence' the ordinary principles of historical scholarship and the handling of documents must apply. This is a matter for specialists and need not be discussed here. But peculiarly literary methods, such as the use of stylistic criteria, are often involved; and there are questions about their status.

E. K. Chambers objects to the stylistic disintegrators of Shakespeare, 'that the sense of style is itself ultimately dependent on external evidence. There is no way of getting at the characteristics of an individual writer, except from work of which his authorship is acknowledged. And if the acquired sense is then used to discredit the canon wholesale, a vicious circle is set up, of which the inevitable result is chaos.'[1]

If the discrediting of the canon is sufficiently wholesale to cut away most of the evidence on which the sense of style was based, then clearly Chambers is right. But it is often necessary to use less extreme forms of this procedure; and in less extreme forms the circle may not be vicious but benign. The method may have been badly used, but in principle there is nothing wrong with it. On the most pessimistic estimate more of what is in the Shakespeare canon is by Shakespeare than by anyone else. We can thus quite properly form a sense of Shakespeare's style from the canon as it stands, even though it is imperfect. And on this basis we can dispose of passages that seem anomalous.

Arguments of this kind must always fall short of certainty; they have been a happy hunting-ground for mania and aberration; but they are in themselves a perfectly respectable branch of that part of literary scholarship that is concerned with establishing matters of fact.

Alarm and despondency are sometimes felt by literary persons at the use of computers, etc., in examining stylistic matters. Surely this is an unnecessary panic. The machines can furnish quickly and accurately evidence that could only be acquired laboriously and uncertainly by other methods. But the evidence has to be interpreted; and the interpretation is always a subject for human judgment and the human sense of relevance.

It is true that such methods may acquire an unwarranted prestige and be thought to settle by themselves matters which they cannot settle. This is not because the machines are getting on top of us, but because of our stupidity, cowardice or superstitious respect in handling them, and their keepers.

---

[1] *William Shakespeare*, 1930, I, 220.

An Essay on Criticism

173. Much of the preliminary work of criticism, much even of the substance of criticism, is descriptive. Before a work can be interpreted or judged it must be correctly described. And this descriptive part of criticism can also be regarded as a factual matter. Since all the relevant facts are open to inspection in the work itself, between two candid and adequately trained readers there should be no cause for disagreement. And commonly there is not. Disagreement begins later, in the realm of interpretation and value judgment. The views of C. S. Lewis and F. R. Leavis on Milton were notoriously divergent; but we find Lewis writing: 'Dr. Leavis does not differ from me about the properties of Milton's epic verse. He describes them very accurately. . . . It is not that he and I see different things when we look at *Paradise Lost*. He sees and hates the very same that I see and love.'[1]

What makes it appear otherwise is that criticism, which owes no particular allegiance to scientific method, often mingles description with interpretation and value judgment. This is indeed the natural manner of literary discourse; but in cases of controversy it is always a great gain to have an unambiguous description that can be agreed on first, even if it can only be achieved by reducing description to a fairly elementary state.

It must be admitted that a full description of a complex work, even if it sets out to be no more than description, often seems to involve interpretation and judgment, and it is only by a somewhat reductive concordat that agreement on a proper description can be reached.

Perhaps something ought to be said here about 'analysis'. But what is called critical analysis, or 'close reading', is in fact only the combination of description with interpretation and value judgment that has been mentioned above. To call it 'analysis' gives it a sort of claim to certainty that it cannot sustain. It is however only the informal method that critics have always employed, but now used with more ingenuity and more minuteness.

Many apparent disagreements in describing the same

[1] *Preface to Paradise Lost*, 1942, p. 130.

object are due to varying degrees of technical sophistication. An inarticulate reader or one unused to formulating his literary impressions in a scholastic context may respond deeply and appropriately to a poem but be capable only of giving a very imprecise description of it. The mere technique of literary description has advanced considerably in the last forty years, and modern critics are in general more accomplished in this respect than their predecessors. They are not always better critics. Older critics often took the facts of literary description for granted, or assumed that there was general agreement about them. And a reader can often be directed more effectively into the right path by general indications than by telling him where to put his foot at every step.

174. A still larger sector of critical discourse is not directly concerned with matters of fact but depends on matters of fact—as a discussion of the development of Shakespeare's style depends on a correct dating of his plays. The obvious thing to say is that if the factual premises turn out to be wrong the conclusions drawn from them are likely to be wrong too. And often they are. In the Shakespeare case above they would have to be. But criticism has a disconcerting habit of breaking loose from its factual premises. We find many instances of just and illuminating critical judgments apparently based on factual evidence that is imperfect or even false.

What happens here is that the apparent premises are not real premises, but only rhetorical starting-points or bits of confirmatory evidence that can be discarded without too much loss. The critical judgment is ultimately validated by reference to the work itself, and the 'external evidence' from which it started has only been introduced in deference to some alien idea of method. John Crowe Ransom suggests in his essay on *Lycidas*[1] that the poem was written smooth and

---

[1] 'A Poem Nearly Anonymous', in *The World's Body*, 1938.

rewritten rough. Fredson Bowers examined the corrections in the manuscript and found that the reverse was the case.[1] Yet Ransom's suggestion is by no means valueless. It must be restated. Whatever the chronology of the actual writing as revealed in the MS (and MSS at best only reveal a late stage in the creative process) *Lycidas* contrives to suggest an ideal of perfect formal and metrical smoothness to which it deliberately refuses to conform.

When an acceptable critical judgment apparently depends on evidence that turns out to be false we must redraft the argument so that the conclusion no longer depends on this evidence. The experienced reader of criticism does this quite often in his own mind, almost without realizing it—which suggests that the role of ascertainable external facts in establishing critical judgments is often smaller than might be supposed.

This does not excuse the too-frequent literary habit of continuing to base critical judgments on evidence that has been shown to be quite unreliable. Criticism has a particularly bad record in this respect, and literary critics are probably more cavalier and unscrupulous in their handling of factual evidence than the learned in any other field. For about three hundred years critics cited the 'three unities of Aristotle' as authoritative dramatic rules; but it hardly seems to have occurred to anyone to look up the text of the *Poetics* to see if they were really there, or if what was there was really presented as a 'rule'.

It is a mistake in criticism to cite factual evidence external to the work under consideration unless the argument really requires it. But in criticism, as in other branches of knowledge, if it is cited it had better be right.

175. The greater part of critical discourse however is composed of statements that are not subject to factual verification,

[1] *Textual and Literary Criticism*, Cambridge, 1959, p. 3.

and cannot be true or false in any simple sense, but only more or less helpful. Interpretation soon becomes a question of what weight is to be attached to a particular element in a work; of how the elements might be related to each other; of the determination of an emotional tone; of the significance of metaphors and symbolic constructions; of the moral deductions to be drawn from a fictional train of events. Questions of value reach the state illustrated by Lewis—'Dr. Leavis sees the same things as I do but what he hates I love.' Or interpretations and value judgment may be confusingly linked: what one critic reads as a failed realistic narrative another reads as a successful romance.

Few of these matters can be determined with certainty; yet we feel that they are open to rational argument. How are such arguments conducted?

176. One method is that of casuistry, in the proper sense of the word—the application of general principles to special cases. A general principle such as that of unity, required or supposed to be required of all literary works, is applied to the work under consideration. In the days when the old theory of fixed kinds was in full vigour this method was more used than it is today. A tragedy was judged by its correspondence with the known idea of tragedy; and so on. For reasons that we have already outlined this sort of judgment is less prevalent in modern literature. But it is by no means extinct.

Since the Romantic period the casuistry has tended to become more subtle, and the rights of the individual case tend to be felt more strongly than those of the general principle. It is even said that criticism should not be the application of general principles at all. But surely this is wrong. A great deal of rational and useful literary discourse is precisely the applying of general principles to special cases. The principles are not in doubt. (There are many critical principles, far more than is often supposed, that are not really disputed by anyone; we all know that order is better than chaos.) The difficulty lies in the application to the special cases. Does the work in question really come under the principle invoked, or is the principle in this case not relevant? Does the work satisfy the principle perhaps in some devious or unobvious way? These questions can be open to rational argument, but often not to certain solutions. We can disagree at first, but we may be persuaded; we can disagree and continue to disagree about the special case, even though there is perfect agreement about the general principle.

177. If argument from general principles has tended to decline in importance, another kind of argument has correspondingly increased. That is argument by analogy or comparison; and it is today probably the most versatile and serviceable tool that criticism has at its disposal. It is used both in interpretation and in value judgment. It is chiefly by a widening circle of comparisons that order is brought into our literary experience.

We interpret a play of Shakespeare by comparing it with other plays of Shakespeare, by noting analogous patterns and similar distributions of emphasis in a number of plays. We interpret the plays of Shakespeare in general by comparing them with those of other dramatists of his time: we know more about Shakespeare when we can see how his aims and procedures differ from Jonson's. And we tend continually to extend the range of comparison beyond the historically adjacent. We interpret Elizabethan drama partly by seeing it in the light of other dramaturgies—the Greek, for example, to which it is not historically related. An English reader comes to understand Racine by comparing him with Shakespeare and noting the differences in intention and method.

A large part of literary interpretation, then, is argument by analogy. We come to understand the morphology of one literary work by understanding the morphology of many others; and our understanding is increased in proportion to the range, variety and relevance of the comparisons we are able to make. Sometimes the comparisons are explicit, sometimes they contribute silently towards the forming of an interpretation but disappear before it is actually expressed, or survive only as brief allusions.

What is vulgarly called name-dropping in the work of wide-ranging critics is not always so; it is a means of orienting a discussion by established points of reference. And it is no use telling students that they gain more from the study of a single work 'in depth' than they do from wide reading. A work cannot be studied deeply without seeing it in relation to other works, and wide reading is a necessary concomitant of deep reading.

178. However, to understand a literary work by seeing that it is like another, or significantly different, does not in itself help us towards judgments of value. Comparison helps us towards value judgments only where there are some fixed points of reference, some works whose value is not in doubt.

In practice there are such works—those of Homer, Dante and Shakespeare, for example. They tend to be regarded as absolutes. We situate certain kinds of narrative by reference to Homer, certain kinds of drama by reference to Shakespeare; and we do not feel any need to argue about Homer and Shakespeare.

But even when the points of reference are less certainly placed they can be used. For example, A wants to argue that Priestley's *Good Companions* is a great novel, gives as his ground that it is just like Dickens, and says that if B disapproves of it he is committed to disapproving of Dickens too. B has three possible answers.

(a) He may be convinced, and say yes, Priestley is like Dickens; I must try to see more in him because I admire Dickens.

(b) He can say yes, Priestley is like Dickens, but Dickens is not a great novelist anyway. In this case the comparison will not have done anything to advance the argument and another will have to be found. What about Balzac?

(c) He can say that Dickens is indeed a great novelist, but Priestley is not like him. He will then have to demonstrate the unlikeness; a useful differentiation will be made, A's literary education will be improved, and the argument can go forward.

Such arguments do not guarantee a right answer. The second answer is inconclusive, and the first is wrong. It will require a different set of tools to differentiate between Priestley and Dickens; but in the end someone will probably turn up to do it. At least a method of making some critical headway is offered.

In actual practice arguments about literary value are less painfully simple than this; but they often take this form. Commonly enough some relevant work or class of works can be found whose value is agreed by both sides; and the work in question can be usefully compared to it. Even if such arguments are not decisive they at least focus attention on the work, not on miscellaneous irrelevancies, and they often advance the argument a step further. Naturally, the wider the disputants' literary interests and knowledge the more fruitful such discussions are likely to be. Those who have a large stock to draw on are more likely to find comparisons that fit. Indeed it will be found that critics with wide and catholic literary interests are less likely than others to disagree in their value judgments. Disagreements about literary value are often the result of narrow and incompatible ranges of interest.

Authoritative criticism derives its authority from being based on a wide range of comparisons. This is not a matter of mere knowledge, reposing inertly as in an encyclopaedia; to provide valuable comparisons a critic's knowledge must be active and interrelated. A good critic is continually increasing the complexity and interrelation of his literary knowledge, and this does not make his task more intricate, but simpler.

Judgments and interpretations become surer and more rapid because they are analogous to judgments and interpretations that have already been made. It is in the activity and inter-relation of his literary knowledge that a critic chiefly differs from a man of learning without critical interests.

179. How is the judgment of those works that are taken as universal standards of comparison arrived at? Ultimately as Johnson said it was: by common consent over a long period of time. This common consent has difficulty in crossing the major cultural boundaries—that between Europe and China, for example; and it is probably only valid within a culture that is freely and naturally integrated. It is a disturbing reflection that its validity may be threatened by the power of modern methods of cultural manipulation. No one has worked or conspired to cause Shakespeare to be accepted as the greatest of dramatists. The consent to this judgment has been freely given. Today cultural imperialism and sheer commercial interest attempt to engineer such judgments. If enough Fulbright professors go around the world saying that Hawthorne is as good as Dostoievski, if you pay enough copywriters to say that Saul Bellow is a great novelist, many people will come to believe it. Great novelists, like great painters, are created today by advertising and a rigged market. It will in the future require more faith than it did in the past to trust to the common consent of mankind. We do not know the outcome of this situation, for it is new. But we must continue to suppose, until it is proved otherwise, that the process is self-regulating, that time corrects all balances, and that the effects of political and cultural brain-washing do not last for ever.

180. Often the actual process of literary discussion is carried on not by adducing new knowledge, but by reminding hearers or readers of what they know already—the existence and nature of works relevant for comparison; obvious descriptive features; moral commonplaces. The number of possibly relevant considerations in a literary argument is very great, and the right ones may not be immediately present to the mind. The critic's task is often to recall to mind things that everybody knows, at the right time and in the right context. In this way a fuller interpretation, an altered or more reliable judgment may be arrived at without the introduction of any new concepts or any new facts.

This is true of other studies, too, but more markedly of criticism. A mistaken notion of 'research' and mistaken analogies with the natural sciences tend to bring about a fruitless search for critical novelty. The result is either mere eccentricity or the accumulation of irrelevant information on which no critical conclusions can really be based.

When we are reminded, in the manner described above, interpretation or judgment may be modified and agreement reached. But we may continue to feel that what we have been reminded of is irrelevant, or not of sufficient weight to change the situation much. Still, something will have been gained; we shall know more exactly the nature of the disagreement—A attaches great weight to a certain factor to which B does not. The best possible situation is where the participants in a discussion are each able to enrich and correct the other's point of view by relevant reminders. The worst is where the reminders are inept, and so many red herrings are drawn across the trail that all ends in a confused smell.

181. Can we say anything about the method by which these familiar but absent considerations are brought to bear at the right moment? Not much. There are no rules for it. It is partly a matter of literary experience, and partly (to let in at

last those secret agents we have kept off as long as possible)
a matter of taste, tact and character on the part of the critic.
What, it will be said, criticism is 'just a personal matter' after
all? Then what has all this argument been about? In a sense it
is a personal matter; but not in the sense that critical judgments are 'just a matter of taste'. To say that criticism is
personal is not to reduce it to an anarchy of individual preferences. In principle literary judgments are objective; some
things are really better than others. But the degree of certainty with which judgments can be enforced, the methods
used to arrive at them, and the persuasiveness of the arguments employed are very much a matter of the critic's
personal equipment and personal style. And this is the more
marked because there is no standard form for literary arguments; and because critics are men of letters rather than
philosophers or scientists, and commonly employ a literary
rhetoric, with all its richness, variety and uncertainty. We feel,
rightly I believe, that any attempt to reduce critical discourse
to formal dialectic or scientific method would lose more in
comprehensiveness and sensitivity than it could possibly gain
in rigour.

182. It is said that if a critical argument is carried far enough
it always turns into an argument about something other than
literature; and, it is often implied, about something more
fundamental—politics or religion. This is probably true; but
it is the critic's business to postpone the translation as long
as possible. Unskilled literary discussion quickly short-
circuits literature and becomes an ideological wrangle; but it
is part of the accomplishment of the critic to keep the discussion as long as possible in literary terms, where irreducible
oppositions are relatively few and there is a considerable body
of case-law that is necessarily accepted by both sides.

Irreducible oppositions are relatively few because literary
discussions do not involve our material interests; nor, rightly

interpreted, our conative dispositions or our metaphysical ends. There is much that is necessarily accepted by both sides because the broad outlines of literary history are matters of established fact that cannot be disputed by anyone; and this undeniable history carries with it at least the sketch of a system of values. It is not really open to anyone to say 'Yes, Dante's works exist, but they are not of any importance.' This is contradicted by a large body of indisputable evidence. And it would be a very strange position to hold that Dante's fame and influence were no evidence of his literary merit. Literary argument proceeds from a number of fixed positions—positions established empirically by 'length of duration and continuance of esteem'. Perhaps their number is not very great, if literary nationalism and period taste are taken into account; but it is sufficient to give literary discourse a fair degree of stability. For these reasons we are more likely to agree about literature than about religion, or political and social ends.

When the argument extends beyond literature it is true that we often arrive at irreducible disagreements; but not the least value of literary discussion is that it often works the other way—that it affords common ground to persons whose political or religious principles are irreconcilably opposed. Literary discourse is ultimately a conversation about a shared enjoyment. The arts, like other human activities, are subject to their corruptions; but essentially they are an eirenicon rather than a cause of strife.

INDEX

Abrams, M. H., 77 n., 129, 159

Aquinas, St. Thomas, 17, 70

Ariosto, 20, 29

Aristotle, 9, 10, 11, 24, 42, 43, 46, 82, 83, 84, 105, 140, 159

Arnold, Matthew, 6, 70, 91, 92 n.

Austen, Jane, 114

Balzac, 56

Barfield, Owen, 128

Barthes, Roland, 37 n.

Baudelaire, 21

Baumgarten, A. G., 12, 17

Beardsley, Monroe, 59, 64

Bentham, Jeremy, 97

Bible, 50, 53, 54

Blake, 123 n., 158

Bodkin, Maud, 143 n.

Boswell, 54

Bowers, Fredson, 160

Bradley, A. C., 12, 13

Bradley, F. H., 7

Brontë, Emily, 117

Brooks, Cleanth, 77 n.

Browne, Sir Thomas, 52

Bunyan, 53

Burke, 50, 90

Burns, 77

Byron, 23

Campbell, Joseph, 143 n.

Cassirer, Ernst, 129, 130, 140, 141

Caudwell, Christopher, 36

Chambers, E. K., 164

Chiari, Joseph, 134 n.

Cicero, 98

Cinthio, Giraldi, 20, 21

Coleridge, 16, 17, 46, 103, 105, 106, 123 n., 157, 159

Dante, 70, 79

Divina Commedia, 78

Delfel, Guy, 134 n.

Demosthenes, 98

Dickens, 48, 56, 115, 171

Dryden, 38, 85

Ehrenzweig, A., 22 n.

Eliot, George, 92, 93, 114

Eliot, T. S., 6 n., 80, 109, 117

Empson, William, 41, 73, 136

Engels, Friedrich, 32, 33, 35 n.

Frazer, Sir James, 140, 142

Freud, Sigmund, 46 n., 72, 140

Frye, Northrop, 8, 13, 43 n., 71, 75, 85, 87, 124 n., 148 ff.

Gardner, Helen, 71 n.

Gautier, Théophile, 10, 11

Genet, Jean, 11, 80

Gibbon, Edward, 50, 52, 54

Goethe, 123 n.
  Dichtung und Wahreit, 55
  Wahlverwandtschaften, 23
  Wilhelm Meister, 22
Goldmann, Lucien, 34, 37
Gray, Thomas, 105, 108
  Elegy, 41
Grierson, H. J. C., 64 n.

Haggard, Sir H. Rider, 58
Hampshire, Stuart, 29
Hawthorne, Nathaniel, 112 n.
  153
Hobbes, Thomas, 50
Homer, 21, 70
House, Humphry, 137
Hugh of St. Victor, 69

James, Henry, 16, 17, 112
  The Golden Bowl, 112
  Portrait of a Lady, 119
Johnson, Samuel, 12, 27, 29,
  87, 88, 91 n., 106, 160
Jones, Ernest, 46 n.
Joyce, James
  Dubliners, 100
  Portrait of the Artist, 27
  Ulysses, 37
Jung, C. G., 46 n., 72, 140,
  146

Kant, 12
Keats
  Grecian Urn, 7
Kermode, Frank, 134 n.
Kettle, Arnold, 117, 119
Knight, Wilson, 25

Lamb, Charles, 56
Langer, Suzanne, 129, 141
Lawrence, D. H., 38
  Kangaroo, 113
  The Rainbow, 113
Leavis, F. R., 30, 166
Lehmann, A. G., 134 n.

Lewis, C. S., 64, 123 n., 166
Liddell, Robert, 115 n.
Lowes, Livingstone, 136
Lukacs, G., 11 n., 35 n.

MacLeish, A., 135
Mallarmé, 19, 104, 128
Maritain, Jacques, 13
Marx, Karl, 33
Marxism, 31, 32, 33, 37,
  46, 72
Mill, J. S., 58
Milton, 62
  Lycidas, 62, 153, 167
  Paradise Lost, 83
  Samson Agonistes, 61
Montaigne, 56

Nabokov, Vladimir, 38
Nietzsche, 19 n.

Origen, 74
Ovid, 21, 70

Pater, Walter, 51, 128
Petrarch, 41
Plato, 9, 11, 12, 27, 43, 75,
  82
Plekhanov, G., 33
Poe, E. A., 23, 24, 25, 128
Pope, 103
Pound, Ezra, 23, 24 n., 109
Priestley, J. B., 172

Rabanus Maurus, 69
Racine, 41
Raglan, Lord, 143 n.
Ransom, J. C., 19, 39, 167
Read, Sir Herbert, 100
Richards, I. A., 63, 75, 128
Richardson, Samuel, 35
Righter, William, 87 n.
Rimbaud, 128
Ruskin, 61, 71
  Praeterita, 55

Sainte-Beuve, 36
Sartre, J. P., 4, 33, 37, 80, 134
Schlegel, A. W., 16, 157
Scott, Sir Walter, 113
Shakespeare, 41, 48, 70, 71,
    124, 125, 138, 163, 164,
    173
Shelley, 11, 80
Sidney, Sir Philip, 42, 44
Smalley, Beryl, 69 n., 70 n.
Spencer, Herbert, 58
Spenser, Edmund, 32, 37, 39,
    61
Spicq, C., 69 n., 70 n.
Spitzer, K., 39 n.
Stendhal, 56, 113
Sterne, Laurence
    Tristram Shandy, 21, 22
Stevenson, R. L., 115 n.

Taine, Hippolyte, 36
Tasso, 20, 27, 155
Tillotson, Geoffrey, 68

Tillyard, E. M. W., 63
Tolstoy, 12, 27, 32
Trissino, 20, 83
Trotsky, Leon, 11 n.

Verlaine, 128
Virgil, 70

Warren, R. P., 136
Watson, G., 57 n., 62
Watt, Ian, 70 n.
Wells, H. G., 34, 35
Weston, Jessie L., 143 n.
Willey, Basil, 57 n.
Wilson, Edmund, 134 n.
Wimsatt, W. K., 59, 64
Winters, Yvor, 137
Wittgenstein, Ludwig, 96
Wordsworth, 61, 161, 106,
    108

Yeats, W. B., 123 n., 128
Yonge, C. M., 92, 93